THE MARVELS OF PALMISTRY

Published by
Lotus Press Publishers & Distributors

THE MARVELS OF PALMISTRY

Pt. Gopal Sharma, B.E.
Shastri Bhori Lal Kala

Lotus PRESS
4735/22, Prakash Deep Building,
Ansari Road, Daryaganj,
New Delhi - 110002

Lotus Press : Publishers & Distributors
Unit No. 220, 2nd Floor, 4735/22, Prakash Deep Building,
Ansari Road, Darya Ganj, New Delhi- 110002
Ph.: 41325510, 98118-38000
• E-mail : lotuspress1984@gmail.com
www.lotuspress.co.in

ISBN: 978-81-8382-209-1

Printed & Published by : **Lotus Press Publishers & Distributors,** New Delhi-02

PREFACE

Palmistry is the ancient art of interpreting the lines and marks (which appear and disappear over time) on an individual's hand. This data is unique for every individual and gives an insight into his character and future.

Some believe palmistry is related to physiognomy, the ability to judge a person solely on his facial features, which dates back to 1100 BC.

Palmistry has been prevalent in India over 3,000 years. It is a part of a vast field of study, referred to as *Samudrik Shastra,* which literally means the ocean of knowledge. It was thought to have originated from ancient China approximately 3000 years BC. References to palmistry can also be found in Indian scriptures, from approximately 500 years BC.

Today, palmistry has become popular with those wishing to move towards all things 'New Age'.

Palmistry is divided up into three categories:

1. Chirognomy - study of the shape of the hands.
2. Chiromancy (the true palmistry) - lines and other markings.
3. Dermatoglyphics - study of the skin patterns.

Palmistry is best seen as a dynamic process. The lines of the hand are not carved in stone. Since the lines, mounts and signs of the hand, the palm and the fingers reflect our thinking and behaviour patterns the study of the above gives a definite reading of the person. Just as our thinking and progress in life change, so do the lines and markings physically change over time.

Every hand is a map of a life, and every part of the hand, from the fingertips to the wrist, contains important markers to points on the map. The roads and signposts in our hands are created by our nervous systems. Our palms, fingers and hand postures tell a story about who we are and where we are going in our lives.

This book has been designed for the layman, and hence the language is simple, with illustrations wherever necessary. The following presentation is meant to guide the reader in interpreting the lines and markings of the hand through a generalised, deductive approach.

Authors

CONTENTS

Other Books on

OCCULT SCIENCE

1. Teach Yourself Vaastu **(New)**
2. Reiki The Science of Healing
3. The Marvels of Palmistry
4. Healing Power of Gems
5. Awake Kundalini
6. Learn Meditation
7. Teach Yourself Numerology
8. Teach Yourself Astrology
9. Teach Yourself Graphology
10. Teach Yourself Effectively Feng Shui

Lotus PRESS

Unit No. 220, Second Floor, 4735/22,
Prakash Deep Building, Ansari Road, Darya Ganj,
New Delhi - 110002

CHAPTER-1

INTRODUCTION

Palmistry is the process of foretelling one's future by the imprints on the palm. It is also termed as Chiromancy.

Palmistry is an ancient art that interprets the general characteristics of one's hands, through the study of the lines, their patterns and other formations, which appear on the palms and fingers.

Although the general nature of one's hands does not change, the lines, patterns and formations often do. Palmistry may relate to the physical, emotional, mental and health conditions, behaviour and modes of interaction with others.

Palmistry is in itself a complete science that can forecast the future of an individual authentically. In the modern world, it would be very helpful for a person if his future is known. It would be easier for him to realise his goals and ambitions. For this purpose we need an authentic science that can tell the complete past and to foresee.

Palmistry is an important science that tells us about the future very genuinely. Of course various other branches of astrology deal with the predictions of the future course of an individual, but palmistry goes one step ahead, for the results are very clear and accurate. In the other branches of astrology, the moment of birth is very important but in palmistry, it is the lines and mounts on one's hand that hold the key to one's future.

The small, thick, thin and oblique lines in the palm of a person have the whole future imprinted therein. Palmistry has also contributed to the medical and criminal sciences. The diseases of a person can be easily recognised by an experienced palmistry expert and the finger imprints can be used to identify criminal cases.

Palmists exist all over the world. They help us in the responsibility of making our own decisions and offer comfort to those who visit. The ancient art of palmistry has clearly battled against all odds and taken a well-deserved place in modern times.

It is the purpose of palmistry to teach you how to conquer the ancient art of divination by means of stated rules and not by intuition. These rules work more or less accurately under all circumstances, while intuition is transitory, under the influence of some momentary excitement which develops in very rare occasions, a state of true clairvoyance, never to be fully depended on. Palmistry is a well-established science, which attracts everyone to it, even as a layman. However, like every 'Science', one has to have patience and learn its deep intricacies to get its correct and true meaning.

By charting the astrological correspondences found in the hands and understanding the mythologies of the gods and planets associated with each part of that map it is possible to understand yourself and others by making simple observations about thumb size, finger length, gesture, lines and skin colour.

History of Palmistry

Palmistry and hand analysis have intrigued humans throughout history. Nearly everyone enjoys a free hand reading. Perhaps the earliest interest in hand reading occurred when the cave dwellers left their handprints on cave walls over 12,000 years ago. Throughout history since writing was invented, thousands of documents have been created detailing palmistry and hand analysis techniques.

The *Bible* itself speaks of the markings in one's hand in the book of Job as: "God placed signs or seals in the hands of men, that all men might know their works, and there is always the timeless knowledge that God and nature make nothing in vain." The Hindus, the Greeks, the Christians and many other learned cultures embraced this science of palmistry.

From India, the art of hand-reading spread to other countries, like Tibet, Egypt, Persia and countries in Europe. Palmistry came to China about 3,000 years before the birth of Christ. It progressed well in Greece where Anaxagoras practised it.

According to Hindu philosophy, a person takes birth according to his/her past actions (*karmas*). As human beings differ in shape, features, constitution, etc., so do the lines on the hands, the ridges on the thumb, the papillary lines on the fingers and the thumb of a person not be seen on any other persons. No two hands are alike.

Just as astrologers use the planets to reveal information about a person, the palmist uses a person's hands or more specifically his palms to talk about his past, present and his future.

Palmistry is a very ancient art, especially favoured in the East, but there are also many modern variations brought about by personal experience of palmists involved in research.

Man has sought the means of projecting the future and self-understanding always, and palmistry is an effective and efficient method of achieving this when used by a competent palm reader.

The hand cannot perform a single action without the brain, and there are more nerves from the brain to the hand than to any other part of the body. The hands are the major messaging tools of the human community from time immemorial. Long before languages came into vogue hand gestures played an important role in communications. We write with them, work with them, and touch others with our hands only. Hence many ancient civilisations had good reason to study mankind through the hands—their shape, their texture, and the lines within them.

Since the palm is the gift of nature no errors can be ascribed to the lines on the palm, which are there since birth. Palmistry is a method of counselling that originated in India and China over 3,000 years ago. The Emperor of China used his thumbprint when sealing documents in 3000 BC and the Greek physicians Hippocrates and Galen (AD 130-200) both used palmistry as a clinical aid.

The science of chiromancy or palmistry commenced before Christianity. Esteemed scientists and philosophers such as Aristotle, Pliny, Anaxagoras, Hispanus, Cardamis and Emperor Augustus all subscribed to this fascinating discipline of palmistry.

Palmistry has provoked a diverse number of responses over the years and has been shrouded in mystery since time began. Because of its close connection with Gypsies and Romanies, and the fact there were no real rules or method, it produced immense opposition from the Church. They believed it to be a form of devil worshipping.

The oldest known palmistry work in the English language is a manuscript known as the Digby Roll IV dated 1440. However, many of the oldest writings originate from India.

Information on the laws and practice of hand reading has been found in *Vedic* scripts, the *Bible* and early Semitic writings.

Cheiro is known as the father of palmistry and he wrote several well-known books on palmistry.

Aristotle (384-322 BC) discovered a treatise on palmistry on an altar to the god Hermes.

Julius Caesar (102-44 BC) judged his men by palmistry.

Notable people such as Paracelsus (1493-1541) and Fludd (1574-1637) brought respectability to palmistry through their writings.

Advances in genetics, psychology and forensics have brought palmistry into focus in the modern age. In 1901 Scotland Yard adopted the technique of fingerprinting in criminal investigation and identification. Medical researchers studying skin patterns (dermatoglyphics) have discovered a correspondence between genetic abnormalities and unusual markings in the hand. Research has confirmed a link between specific fingerprint patterns and heart disease.

Palmistry has many systems of interpretation. It is also an intuitive art that is easily learned just by learning a few basics about the symbolism that is represented by the lines that run across the palm, the mounts (or fleshy parts) of the palm and the structure of fingers.

Palmistry is not foretelling. The original intent of palmistry was for personality assessment and counselling. One's emotional tendencies, social attitudes, conscious awareness and subconscious fears, blockages and strengths can be understood in great detail through this indepth system which analyses the hand and the markings it carry. Though these days it is used to predict the future of an individual, palmistry does well with the personality assessment task.

In palmistry, the hand as a whole is divided into three different sections. The fingers represent the mind and the higher self. The middle of the palm represents day-to-day life and the conscious mind. The lower half of the hand represents primal instincts, health and basic drives of the subconscious. Palmistry is all about proportion, symmetry and distortions of what would be considered to be a perfectly formed hand.

It is important to look at both hands during a reading. Depending on which hand is active (usually seen as the hand you write with), in combination with the inactive hand, your hand shows where you have been (passive), and where you are likely to be headed (active) in this life.

In accordance with this fact, it is important not to analyse the left hand like a semi-literate gypsy does but study both palms.

Only such a complex analysis can clarify the main tendencies of a personality development and, as a consequence, can point at what we can expect in the future.

Look at your palms. You can be convinced of a sufficient difference between the picture and the shape of individual elements. Learn these differences, try to imagine what will happen if the further development goes in this direction. Let it be a key to your future cognition, future knowledge.

One of the common questions people ask about palmistry is, what is the difference between reading the right hand and the left hand? Palmists will mostly examine your most active hand that is usually the one you write with. It is this hand that shows your current and future trends. The passive hand in palmistry tends to show your childhood. The main difference consists in that the left hand shows what a person was born with but the right one what kind of a person he has become by the present time. The opposite is true for the left-handers. The thing is that the right hand, used more frequently, accumulates those changes that occur to us during our life.

Palmistry is a marvellous field of science today, having borrowed its assets from the ancient civilisations of all lands. Your palm is your personality. Very few people realise that they are carrying around a full map of their character and potentialities. Besides being a fascinating study, palmistry can help in vocational guidance, health and psychological diagnosis, partnership compatibility, etc.

Each of our fingers and mounds has an astrological correspondence. Did you know that the size of your Saturn finger tells a lot about how you handle responsibility? That you can decide whether someone is giving you an honest deal by looking at the areas of the hand ruled by Mercury? Although the general nature of one's hands does not change, the lines, patterns and formations often do.

Palmistry may relate to the physical state, emotional, mental and health condition, tendencies and modes of interaction with others, or even spiritual aspects of our being. A palmist is capable of providing a client with a range of information concerning his general nature, abilities and potentials. A degree of information regarding his past, present and future may be provided, but for more detail of this kind the palmist needs to use his psychic abilities.

These days palmistry is well accepted throughout the world. Professional palmists can be found reading palms in every country in the world. Pick up almost any copy of a women's magazine and there is some information on palmistry. There are thousands of books written on the subject and there are palmistry clubs the world across.

You may or may not make actual predictions with palmistry. However, since there is a definite mind-body connection, we know that negative or positive thinking affects our well-being. Due to our habitual way of thinking, we often repeat the same behaviour in the future as we exhibit in the present. If we can understand the pattern of our habits and thinking, then we can begin to ignore the negative cycles of behaviour and can replace them with positive ones. Palmistry can help you see these patterns. With this information, you can shape your own destiny.

CHAPTER-2

THE HAND

The study of the general shape of hands, of the fingers, fingernails and their skin texture is termed as Chirognomy. This study helps in finding out the true personality of the individual under study.

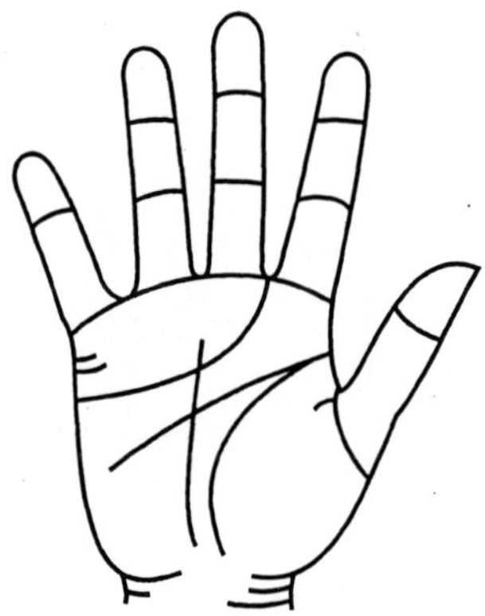

Hand

In some systems, the right hand represents what you are today while the left represents all that you were born with.

Which hand do you read? The left and right hands are totally different from one another. It is very rare to find a pair of palms that are identical. But as a popular practice, it is advisable to read the hand that the person writes with, as that would be considered to be the dominant hand.

The theory behind this is that your potential at birth is revealed in the left hand while the right hand represents your adult self and shows what you have done with your abilities. This is reversed in left-handed people.

In palmistry, you have to study both hands. The hand you write with is your dominant or active hand. It reflects the conscious you. The other hand, the passive or minor hand, is more about the subconscious. So both hands must be considered to see the 'whole' person.

Size of the Hand

The size of the hand can be important in helping to judge your character and personality.

Small Hands

People with small hands have a strong desire to achieve, setting long-range goals in their life. They sometimes have an inflated ego and have trouble relaxing. They like to plan and to manage more than they can execute. They have a lot of energy, and have the ability to command respect as they possess executive power.

Medium-sized Hands

People with medium hands are well balanced and have a good sense of judgement. They have common sense and are practical.

If the fingers as long as the palm, the indication is of a successful businessman, not specialised in any particular kind of business. He is the Jack-of-all-trades-but-master-of-none type.

If the fingers are longer than the palm, then the person with this hand has the ability to grasp things quickly and make big plans. He has a dislike of details though.

If the fingers are shorter than the size of the palm, the indication is of a person who is not good in planning, but can 'finish' everything he is asked to do. He will not neglect even the minutest detail, denoting that he is slow but sure of completion of a project.

Large Hands

People with large hands with small fingers are capable in many respects. They can have many goals, all at the same time. They are friendly and very sociable.

People with large hands and long fingers are fond of details. They are irritable by temperament.

Those with large and narrow hands are more imaginative and idealist than practical. If their hands are long and thin, selfishness is denoted.

Broad Hands

People with broad hands (square type) show common sense and broad-mindedness, exhibit a lot of energy and have a practical and businesslike attitude.

They are kind and sympathetic, and consider both sides of an issue before coming to any conclusion.

Soft Hands

People with soft hands are usually lazy, but full of talents that are not tapped. Those whose hands are moderately soft, or whose mounts only are soft, work in short bursts only.

Very Hard Hands

A person with very hard hands has a lot of energy and loves work for its very own sake. He has to cultivate mental disciplines in order to harness his energies and not allow them to go to waste.

General

Crude hands that are thick, hard and irregular belong to a manual worker.

Small-handed people do things on a large scale; people with big hands do things involving fine detail. But remember, it is relevant to your overall body size.

Hair on the Hands

On most hands you will find little or no hair. Hair is most common on the back of men's hands. Normally, the more hair there is, the more the physical strength indicated.

A profusely hairy hand is often found on men with a high sex drive. They also indulge in overeating, and often in times of crisis will revert to their animal instincts.

People with sparse, fine and thin hair on the back of the hand lack vigour. They often tend to suffer from nervous problems. Although on the good side, people with less hair are more diplomatic. The colour of the hair is important.

Flexibility of the Hands

The degree of flexibility in your hand indicates your emotional and mental health. In short, a flexible hand suggests a flexible mind, a stiff hand shows a stiff mind.

Emotionally, those people with flexible hands adjust well to their environment.

Stiff hands indicate those who have a rigid outlook on life.

A flexible hand that can bend backwards in a graceful arch indicates a mind that can respond quickly. These people can act, think and feel all at once.

A moderately flexible hand is the most common. People with this type of hand tend to be balanced and in control of themselves.

An extremely flexible hand indicates a person who is vulnerable, easily led by others.

A firm type of hand indicates a strong type of person. These people are conservative with their money and feelings.

Joints and Knuckles

People with smooth knuckles are found to be very meticulous about their appearance and their home.

Those with uneven knuckles tend to have a more balanced and calm approach to life.

People with smooth fingers are very receptive to information and their environment. Information is processed intuitively.

When just only the bottom joints are pronounced the individuals conduct their life in an orderly way.

People with both top and bottom pronounced joints are referred to as philosophical thinkers. They tend to analyse information and think before they act.

CHAPTER-3

SHAPES OF HANDS

The type and shape of hand is very important to understand palmistry. It has been broadly classified into ten parts discussed below.

Elementary or Lowest Type Hand

In appearance the hand is coarse and clumsy, with a large, thick, heavy palm, short fingers and short nails. The hand itself is extremely short and barely reaches the base of the first finger. There is very little to be seen on the palm.

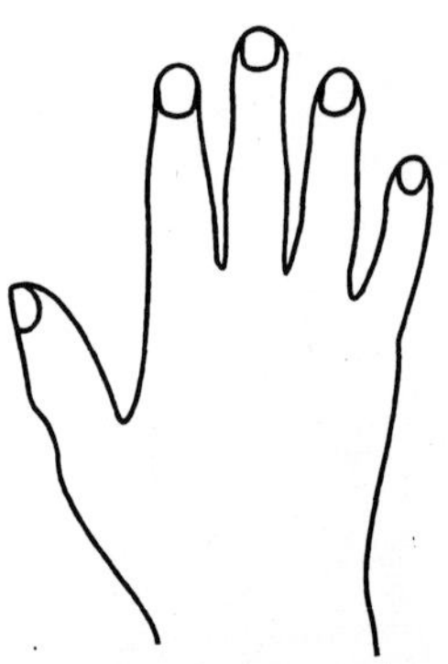

Elementary Hand

Persons with an elementary hand display a lack of enthusiasm and imagination. They show a general indifference to life, and are concerned only with their daily mundane existence. They are largely intolerant of a nasty situation, and can get violent when provoked.

They possess a certain low cunning instinct. These are people without aspirations — they simply eat, drink, sleep, and die.

Mainly labourers possess such a type of hand. Many are also are involved in violent sports, like boxing.

The Square or Useful Hand

People with a square hand have a square palm, a square wrist, square at the base of the fingers, and the fingers and nails are also square. This hand is characterised by a large thumb.

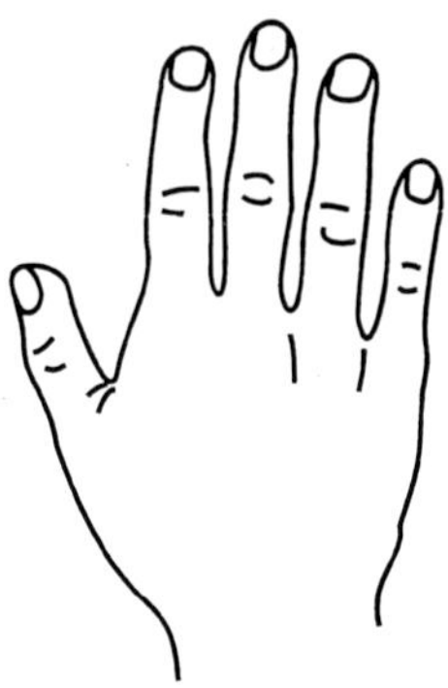

Square Hand

People with square hands are the most practical and logical of all the types. They are orderly, very punctual, and precise in manner. They are honest and reliable, and like to lead disciplined lives, but little imagination. They respect law and order and also authority; they love discipline, and are slaves to custom. They are not quarrelsome, but are determined in opposition. They prefer reason to instinct, peace to war, and are methodical in work and habit.

They are fond of the exact sciences and practical studies. They encourage agriculture and commerce; they love home and the duties of home. They are sincere and true in promises, staunch in friendship, strong in principle and honest in business.

These persons are mainly businessmen, executives, lawyers, doctors, scientists and engineers.

The Spatulate or the Nervous Active Type Hand

People with the fingers of their hand flattened like a spatula have a rather strange characteristic feature: a large thumb. It is extremely broad near the base and tapers towards the fingers, usually found to be crooked and irregular.

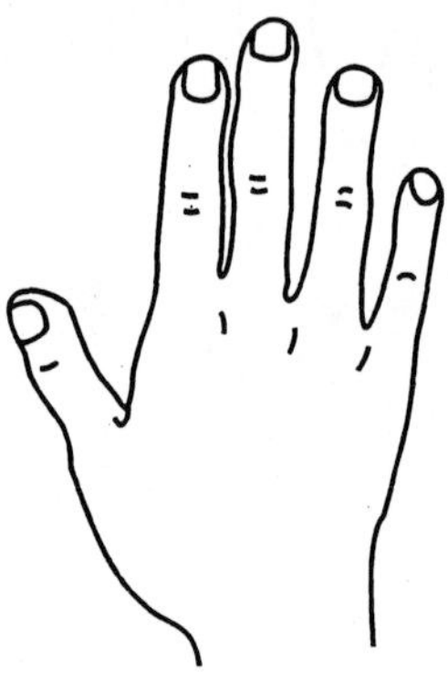

Spatulate Hand

The most striking characteristic is the singular independence of spirit. It is this spirit that makes most people with spatulate hands explorers and discoverers. This is probably why they also to depart from the known rules of engineering and machines to seek the unknown, and thus become famous for their inventions. They have a quest for knowledge, and a restless and excitable nature. They are energetic and dexterous, daring to take risks.

These people are highly individualistic. A singer, actress, doctor, or preacher with such a instinct will break all rules of precedent–not by any means for the sake of eccentricity, but simply because they have an original way of looking at things.

People with this hand are mainly artisans, inventors, explorers, navigators, astronauts, and engineers.

The Conical or Artistic Type Hand

A person with such a hand has smooth fingers, with the nails of shaped like cones, giving the hand its name. The palm is broad, thick and large, and the thumb is also unusually huge.

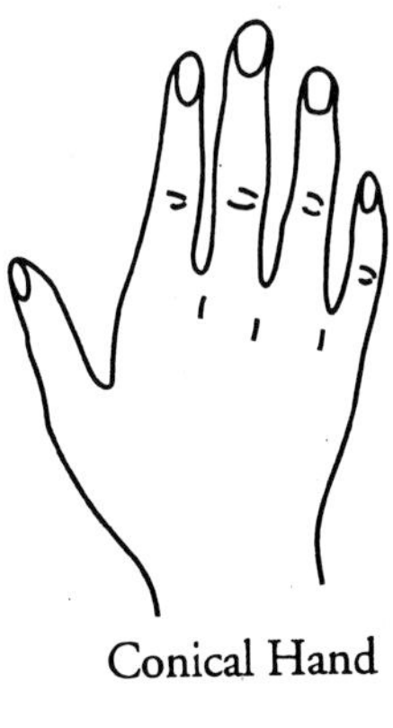

Conical Hand

People with a conical hand are impulsive and have strong instincts. They have an artistic, impulsive nature. They may be clever and quick in thought and ideas, yet they are so utterly short of patience and tire so easily, that they rarely carry out their intentions.

People with this hand are usually connoisseurs of the arts with superb communication skills, living life on a purely sensual level. They judge everything by impulse and instinct. They are also very easily swayed by the people with whom they come in contact, and very much influenced by their surroundings. They carry their likes and dislikes to extremes. They are usually short-tempered but soon cool down. They are generous and sympathetic, but equally selfish where their own personal comfort is concerned.

People with this hand are mainly in the creative field, like painters, sculptors, musician and poets.

The Philosophic or Intellectual Hand

A philosophic hand is long, narrow, and delicate, with slender, tapering fingers and long, almond-shaped nails. The very fact that it is fine and beautiful, however, indicates its lack of energy and strength.

People with such hands are found mainly in India. They are likely to be students of a particular subject. They are philosophers and gain great success in the form of wealth.

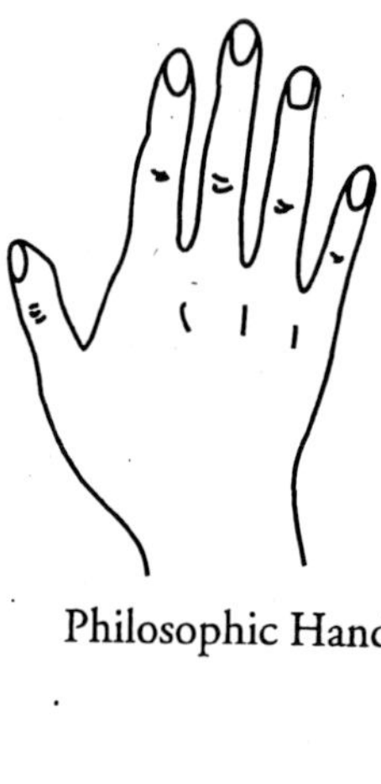

Philosophic Hand

These people are religious by nature. Their passion is to study mankind. They like to be distinct from others, and for this they will go through all kinds of privations. They love mystery in all the things.

People with such hands are generally egotistical, which is in keeping with the life they lead. Joints in the hand that are developed are a characteristic of thoughtful people, while the smooth, pointed fingers are opposite to that. It is the combination of these almost opposite characteristics that brings about the peculiar ideas that such men and women possess.

People with this hand mainly belongs to the profession of teachers, thinkers and world leaders.

The Psychic or Idealistic Hand

A person with a small and slender hand, characterised by smooth fingers is known to be psychic and idealistic. The palm is medium in size, and the phalanges with nails are long and tapering, while the thumb is small and elegant.

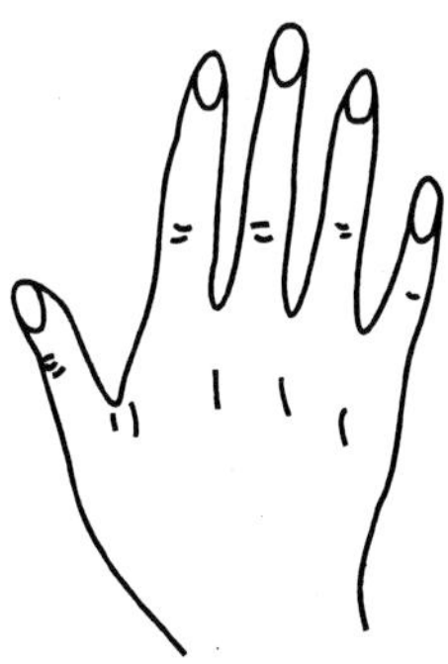

Psychic Hand

This is a most beautiful but unfortunate hand. People with this hand have a visionary and idealistic nature.

This type of hand is very rare to find. The fineness and beauty of this hand indicate little energy and strength in its owner, who struggles to hold his own in the battle of life. People with this hand lead a very confused life characterised by a lack of discipline in their life.

They are gentle in manner, quiet in temper, confiding, and being naïve and trusting, they automatically trust somebody who is kind to them. They are very religious by nature and more impressed with the service, music, and ceremony of the sermon. Parents having children with such a type of hand find it difficult to understand how to treat their children.

Such people mainly belong to the profession of magicians and clairvoyants.

The Necessary Hand

A necessary hand, like the spatulate hand, has its fingers looking more or less flattened out spatula. The thumbs are large, with those in which the instinct peculiar to these hands, supported by the promptings of the brain, makes itself the most clearly manifest.

Such people are almost insensible to art or to poetry. They are endowed with a very small share of the instincts that lead to moral instability. They attach themselves to a country for the material benefits.

They are comfortable with manual labour, and it is the same

with all kinds of active exercise. They suffer from the absence of the necessities of life, but not from the absence of the superfluous, for they are only slightly sensual.

The Brutal Murderer's Hand

This type of hand is a gross imitation of the elementary hand, often common in people with uncontrollably violent temper. The hand is characterised by a thick, heavy palm, reddish in tint, and broader than the average; short, awkward and stiff fingers, generally crooked; often spatulate. There are no extraordinary knots to speak of although sometimes the second joint may be clumsy and thick. The thumb has a 'clubbed' first phalange and the second phalange is very much undersized.

The Congenital Idiot's Hand

This is worse than the brutal murderer's or the elementary hand. This hand is so ill-shaped as often to be justly called crippled. The palm is thick, soft, longer than the fingers and generally narrow. This narrowness is increased by the position of the thumb, set very high and only half detached from the side of the hand; very short besides being clumsy and ill-shaped.

Having a status of criminal, or almost in a level with him, one finds the congenital idiot, the half-developed brain, the child for life.

The fingers are hardly more than one-half the normal size; the phalanges are twisted and their tips rounded and shapeless.

The Mixed Hand

The mixed hand is most difficult to describe, for it is a combination of various hands. It is so called because the hand cannot possibly be classed as solely, artistic, useful, necessary, philosophical or elementary.

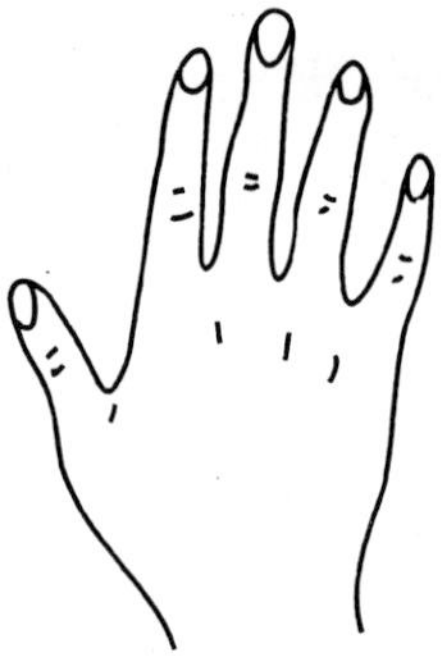

Mixed Hand

The fingers also belong to different types–often one pointed, one square, one spatulate, one philosophic and so on. This is the hand of ideas, of versatility, and generally of changeability of purpose. A person with such a hand is adaptable to both people and circumstances, clever, but erratic in application of his talents.

Apart from the above-mentioned shapes, a few more can be explained.

Ordinary Hand

Such persons are full of practical wisdom. They know how to behave with others. They deal with others in a very practical manner. They get their due respect from the society.

They constantly face struggles in their lives but achieve success. Their health remains good.

They have the greatest capacity of moulding the situations according to the circumstances prevalent around them.

Ideal Hand

This is said to be the best type of hand. This hand is well formed, soft and supple. Such a hand is neither very long nor very wide.

Such persons come to know about their future happenings. They may have to face many troubles in life, but they face them couageously.

They constantly move forward. They are idealistic by nature and are hence far removed from the worldly point of view. Their end is very troublesome.

Female Hand

A female's hands are softer, smoother and more modelled. The characteristics detailed above in the various types of hands can be identified.

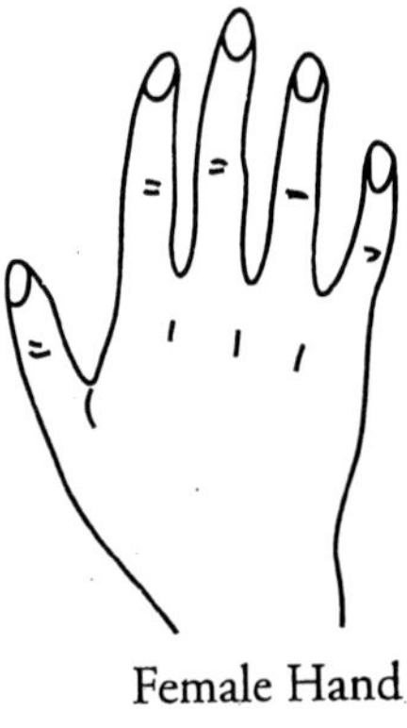

Female Hand

It is rare to find women with elementary type of hands. Very few females are found to possess knotty and spatulate hands. When any of these three characteristics are strongly marked in them, the attributes are present in large measures.

As to having conical or idealistic hands, in many women the hand has something of these features without, however, belonging really to either type.

It is more common to find women with square or mixed type of hands.

Chapter-4

TYPES OF HANDS

There are four basic hand types. These are closely connected with the four elements of the world: Earth, Fire, Water and Air.

These are also linked with corresponding character traits.

Practical–Earth

Signs: Taurus, Virgo and Capricorn.

This hand comprises a square palm with short fingers. Hard working, honest and down to earth.

Intuitive–Fire

Signs: Leo, Aries and Sagittarius.

This hand has a long palm with short fingers. If you have a fire hand you tend to be energetic and restless.

Sensitive–Water

Signs: Cancer, Scorpio and Pisces.

This palm is long with long fingers. Key words include imaginative, emotional and sensitive.

Intellectual–Air

Signs: Gemini, Libra and Aquarius. Air signs are clever, forward thinking and have square palms with very long fingers.

Now let us deal with each type a little more in detail.

The Air Hand

The air hand has a square palm with long fingers. The lines on the palm tend to be thin and the prints are usually loops.

Air Hand

People with an air hand are good at making conversations and at writing. They have a cheerful and happy disposition. They often end up working in the communication industry.

They need constant intellectual stimulation and have a low boredom threshold. People with air hands are good communicators, are popular and often work in the area of media.

The Water Hand

Water hand people have a palm that is rectangular with long fingers. There are a large amount of fine lines on the palm.

The prints are also usually loops. Many people with this hand make good poets and musicians. They also do well in the fashion and beauty industry.

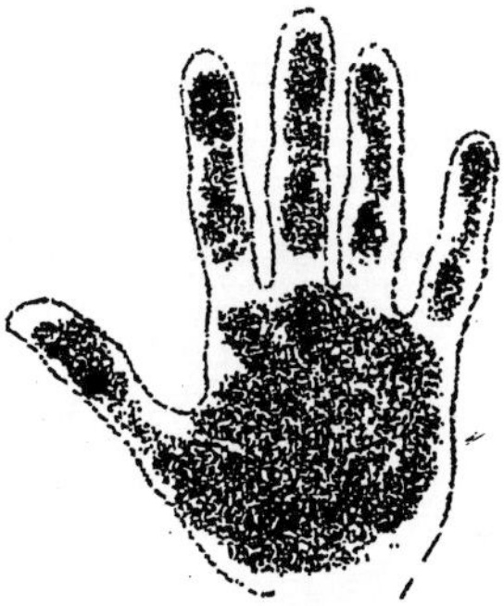

Water Hand

People with this hand focus more on emotions than reason.

The Earth Hand

People with an earth hand have square palms with short fingers. Their palms have usually few lines and there are often arches on the fingertips.

Earth Hand

People with this hand do not much care for change. They tend to be slow in nature and have a strong affinity to nature and have a strong affinity to nature and nature's bounty.

They are emotionally stable and make the best workers. It is an interesting fact that People with earth hands are often successful artists and photographers.

Most people with trade jobs, such as a carpenter, have earth hands. It should also be noted that if they have an earth-shaped hand they would like the countryside and often make good farmers or at least gardeners. These people like stability and become stressed in times of change.

The Fire Hand

The fire hand has a long palm and short fingers. People with this shaped hand tend to be energetic, outgoing and often extroverts.

They are excitable and emotional. They like to be at the helm of affairs and control other people.

There are always a large number of strong lines on the hands and usually whorl fingerprints.

Fire Hand

Fire handed people tend to have a lot of injuries and accidents.

CHAPTER-5

THE PALM

The palm is composed of small bones. There are nearly 14 bones joined together which give shape to the palm. In the front part of these bones there are three more pieces of bones composing each finger and two more composing each thumb. The upper ends of the bones are protected with nails.

The palm extends from the base of fingers and the thumb to the first bracelet on the wrist. The part of the hand on the other side of the palm is called the back of the hand. From the wrist up to the end of the finger of Saturn is termed as 'Hand'.

All the lines on the palm however big or small, thick or thin, are helpful in determining the speed of the life force of the individual. Therefore, it is necessary for an expert palmist to make a critical study of each line found on the palm.

The clear and deep long lines on a palm indicate success, while the broken, thin and indistinct lines are a handicap for the person. Every person has 7 main lines and 12 secondary lines.

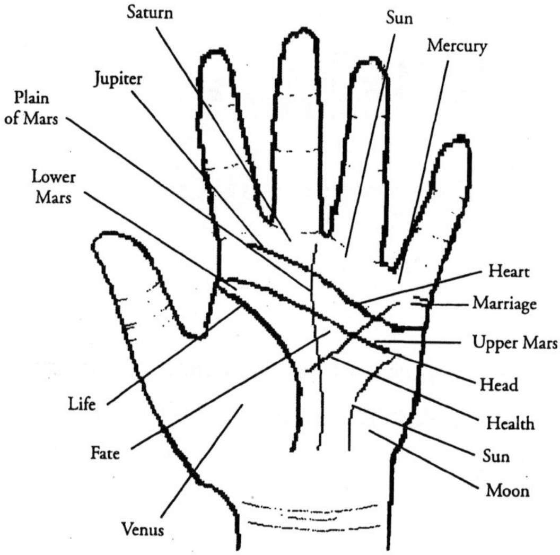

Size and Shape

Narrow Palm

A person with a narrow palm lacks imagination, pluck and cheerfulness, on account of the small space allowed for the development of the three mounts along the percussion–Mercury, Mars and the Moon.

Wide Palm

If the palm is in good proportion with the size and character of the fingers, it is an indication of strong health and evenly balanced temper.

Too Wide Palm

In such a case the palm is generally thick, therefore the exaggeration of the Mounts of the Moon, Mars and Mercury will result in a vicious imagination, a violent temper and deceiving instincts.

Square Palm

This type of palm generally has spatulate fingers, and possesses a great love of activity, mostly of a physical nature.

Teacher's Square

This little square that is just under the index finger is a common sign found among people who work in the teaching profession. It doesn't always mean that the person is a schoolteacher.

It is in fact found also in people who teach anything, whether he is paid or voluntary.

CHAPTER-6

THE SKIN AND TEXTURE

The health of a person is often indicated by the colour of his hands.

Dead white hands often indicate a lack of circulation. White colour denotes a lack of interest in the outside world and those with whom the bearer may associate. White hands denote that the persons are egotistical, resulting in selfishness and a lack of sympathy for others. It is also a symbol for general ill health and weakness.

In palmistry, pink hands denote a sign of good health. Pink hue in the palm denotes a hopeful, sanguine, enthusiastic, and bright nature. A pink and mottled skin is a sign of hopeful, cheerful disposition and a well balanced constitution.

One may consider it to be a less extreme manifestation of a red hand or line. This is the optimal colour for any line in a healthy and well-adjusted person.

Red indicates a great robustness. A red hand will be passionate, quick-tempered, and ardent. This extreme vivaciousness, however, may end in apoplexy. A red line will indicate much of the same, but it will be modified by the function of the line, i.e., a red Line of Life will indicate a vigorous, robust health coupled with an active nature, while a red line of heart will denote overflowing and heartfelt emotions.

Bluish hands indicate a sluggish condition of the circulation of the blood supply.

Yellow in the palm is the mark of the melancholy and morose character. This points towards a morbid disposition and biliousness.

Black lines denote the person to be grave, haughty, distant, and vengeful.

The normal colour of the palm should be rosy and pinkish.

A very pale skin is an indication of selfish disposition and anemia.

Texture of Skin

The skin texture on the hand shows the person's natural refinements. The following are the different types of textures the reader may encounter whilst practising palmistry reading.

Smooth Hands

A person with smooth hands has a very calm and unruffled temperament. Such an individual will rarely lose his temper, and maintain calmness in times of turmoil as well.

Rough Hands

To possess rough hands denotes the opposite. Persons with rough hands have an unpredictable temper that gets roused easily at the slightest provocation. Such individuals usually are more coarse and earthy, and are more fascinated with the concrete than abstract ideas. Lined hands, that is, hands that are networked with a large amount of fine lines, reveal a person who is fretful, worrisome, and easily vexed.

Soft Hands

One who possesses soft hands is generally slothful. Though an individual may possess brilliant markings designing great talent, if the hand is soft, he will find motivation difficult, and perseverance even more so. These hands have a tendency for sensuality.

Firm Hands

Firm hands denote a great deal of energy and drive, also an active nature. Those with firm hands will start many projects, often simultaneously, and possess the energy and follow through to see them to their end.

Hard Hands

If a person has hard hands that are not springy but bony and tough, he lacks energy and enthusiasm. This lacking differs from soft, fleshy hands, however: in the case of soft hands, the individual possesses the energy, but it goes to waste through laziness; in hard hands, there is no energy to begin with. It means a dispassionate, selfish, and potentially pessimistic nature.

Lined Hands

When the hands are networked with a large amount of fine lines, it reveals that the person is fretful, worrisome, and easily vexed or angered.

Naturally, a hand may possess a combination of the above qualities, for it is possible to have a soft, smooth hand or a hard rough hand.

Extra Smooth Skin

Also termed as "satin skin" people possessing such a skin type have a tendency to rheumatism and gout.

Dry Skin

People with a dry skin type are prone to fever, and as perspiration is insufficient there is every likelihood of skin diseases.

Damp Skin

In such a case, especially if the sweat is cold and clammy, it is an indication of very serious liver trouble; often ill-balanced moral nature.

Some more interesting facts on the texture of the skin are given below.

a) If the texture is soft and delicate it will indicate a refined and sensitive person.

b) A transparent skin is found on saintly type of people.

c) Thin skin is found on the hands of overly sensitive people.

d) Often those with a thick skin are stubborn and insensitive.

e) Coarse skin is found on the hands of earthy people.

f) People with a satin-smooth type of skin are very artistic and often have a love of nature.

Qualities of Lines

When diagnosing the importance of a line, the colour, length, and direction are not enough. Often the manner in which the line is etched into the palm will indicate its overall power. The manner in which the lines are engraved on the palm can be described as under.

a) A deeply cut line strengthens the influence of the line over other traits. The deepest line on a palm signifies the most important aspect of their life, i.e., a deeply-cut Line of Heart would designate an emotional, passionate person, while a deep Line of Head would betray an individual enamoured with ideas and the intellect.

b) A thin line indicates the opposite of a deeply cut line as would be expected. A thin line will have little influence over the bearer's life, just as a thin Line of Fate would show little direction in life and a thin Line of Life would show weakness of constitution and health.

c) A broad and shallow line is also a sign of weakness, but typically due to physical factors, either congenital or incidental.

d) A normal line is straight, firm, light pink in hue, and clearly marked on the palm. It denotes a normal and average person.

e) Apart from the primary and secondary lines, there may be lines of chance and influence that rise and fall. One may ascertain whether a line is rising or falling by the varying thickness of a line.

Chapter-7

THE FINGERS

Finger Settings

Personality traits, such as strength of character, may be found from the way the fingers are set into the palm.

People with evenly set fingers are rare, but when found, they indicate confidence. These people always go on to be successful in life.

An uneven setting indicates a person with a lack of self-confidence, especially if the little finger is very low set.

A person with an arched setting will have a well-balanced personality.

Palmistry treats the thumb as a separate entity, which is honoured with a separate and distinct treatment as playing a considerable part in the economy of the hand. Therefore we shall deal with the following fingers before proceeding with the thumb.

1. The First Finger (Index Finger): Finger of Jupiter.
2. The Second Finger (Middle Finger): Finger of Saturn.
3. The Third Finger (Ring Finger): Finger of Apollo.
4. The Fourth Finger (Little Finger): Finger of Mercury.

All these fingers have their own mounts, which are located on the palm right below each one. The more developed or pronounced these fleshy mounds are beneath the finger, the more developed that trait is in a person.

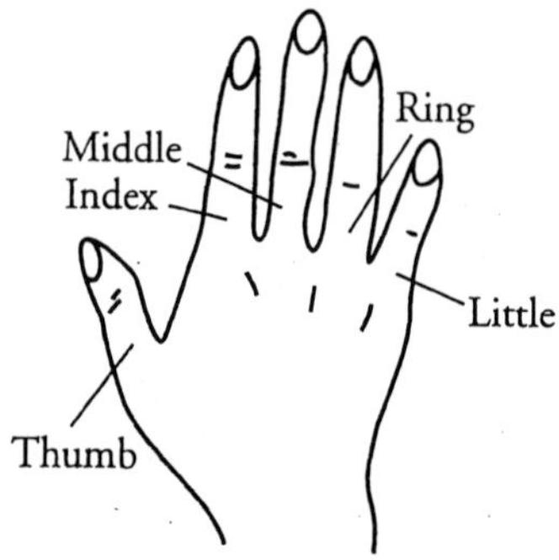

The Fingers

Index Finger

The first finger, next to the thumb, is called the index finger, or Finger of Jupiter. It represents the ego of a person and his desire for recognition or prestige.

The index finger correlates to the planet Jupiter and indicates good fortune and career.

Since ancient times the index finger is said to have normal length if the tip reaches the middle of the nail of the middle finger. If your index finger is longer than the normal length, you tend to be a leader and tell others what to do. If it is shorter however, then you tend to sit back and let others control you.

If the index finger is longer, you can count on a strong Jupiter / Sagittarius. If the index finger is noticeably shorter, the Jupiter will retreat more into the background, or is somehow damaged. This is especially true, if the ring finger is longer than the index finger.

A long index finger shows self-confidence and awareness. It represents the ego of a person and his desire for recognition or prestige. It is indicative of his desire to dominate over others. He is sure of his ability. People with this finger are keen to advance in life. They like to be in charge and have their own way. They are capable and do well being in charge of a crisis situation.

Smaller than normal it represents a lack of ambition. Such a person is only a follower, never a leader.

If a person has a strong index finger that thrusts out on its own it shows a person who likes to lead and make decisions. These people go well as managers. They are good at controlling large amounts of staff.

But if the person has a short index finger it indicates that the person likes to work alone and often become self-employed as a writer or an artist. He is usually shy, afraid he will fail and inclined to have self-doubt.

People with a curved index finger are collectors and often have many hobbies.

Middle Finger

The second finger, next to the Index finger, is called the Middle

Finger, or Finger of Saturn. It represents the balance of mind, sagacity and the love of solitude.

The middle finger represents Saturn / Capricorn.

It is, in most cases, longer than the rest of the digits or fingers. If it is equal in length to the index or the third, or ring finger, it is supposed to be a small middle finger. A person with such a finger will be petty-minded and those having a very long middle finger shy away from human company.

It should always be longer than all the other fingers. Only in this form can one count on having enough sense of responsibility for oneself and toward others. If the middle finger is long it indicates a person who treats life very seriously. He believes strongly in getting ahead.

If the middle finger is remarkably long, broad or heavy, the person suffers from his duties very much. In this case he takes everything too seriously.

People with short middle fingers are careless and generally prefer not to work.

Most people tend to have a middle sized middle finger, meaning they are somewhere in between.

Ring Finger

The third finger, next to the Middle finger, is called the Ring finger, or Finger of Apollo.

The third or the ring finger is indicative of a person's desire for ostentation and fame. It relates to self-expression and intelligence.

A long elegant ring finger always indicates a considerable influence of Venus / Libra, and sometimes also that of an aesthetic constellation of the Sun. If the ring finger is long the persons will have a creative nature. They will go well in the field of art or fashion design. Sometimes this long ring finger is associated with people who have a gambling problem.

If the ring finger is longer than usual, i.e., if it is longer than the index finger, the person would be given to too much ostentation and would love to take risks. Those risks include speculation, gambling and other games of chance.

A person with a small ring finger is totally devoid of the tendency towards ostentation, and persons with such fingers do not take any risks.

Short ring fingers are extremely rare.

Little Finger

The fourth finger is called the Little Finger, or Finger of Mercury. It represents eloquence and wit. It reveals a lot about the ability to communicate.

A little finger which extends to the end of the first phalange of the third finger is considered to be of average length. If it is longer, these qualities become more pronounced in a person. Converse is the case if the finger is of less than average length.

A person with a small little finger suffers from an inferiority complex and he does not have the courage to speak out his mind. A short little finger reveals emotional immaturity.

A longer little finger is regarded as a sign of talent. The person will be able to express himself extremely well. This form speaks of a strong Mercury influence.

He has a high I.Q. People with such a finger make good writers and speakers and have a strong sex drive.

A very short finger set low in the palm indicates childlike behaviour. It indicates the person as a child had a problem with one of his parents. In some cases it indicates he was a victim of child abuse.

If the little finger sticks out from the hand it may indicate the person is involved in a relationship he do not want to be in.

Someone with a thick base of the finger likes a very easy-going and comfortable life. He is very interested in the material and sensual world. The Mercury qualities are said to be normal if the little finger reaches the upper joint of the ring finger. (It's easier to see this on the palm side of the hand.)

If your little finger is shorter than the normal length, it shows that you lack the ability to influence others.

Finger Spacing

Generally the longest finger is about seven-eighths the size of your palm. If they are as long as your palm, then your fingers are considered long.

In relation to the fingers, the thumb is normally higher than the bottom joining of the index finger.

The ring finger normally reaches the base of the nail of the middle finger and the little finger should reach the top joint of the ring finger.

If your little finger stands apart from the ring finger then you tend to be independent.

Planets Associated with Fingers

The little finger
Mercury–reveals health and professional ability.

The ring finger
Apollo–shows fame and fortune.

The middle finger
Saturn–indicates distinction and excellence.

The index finger
Jupiter–symbolises ambition and self-esteem.

The thumb
Shows power and authority.

The Thumb

The thumb is the king of the hand. In a way, it represents the whole hand. Hence more importance is atttached to the thumb than it is given to the lines in the palm. The thumb reveals the whole identity of the individual to the palmist. It is considered as the root of the whole hand, as the centre of the will power.

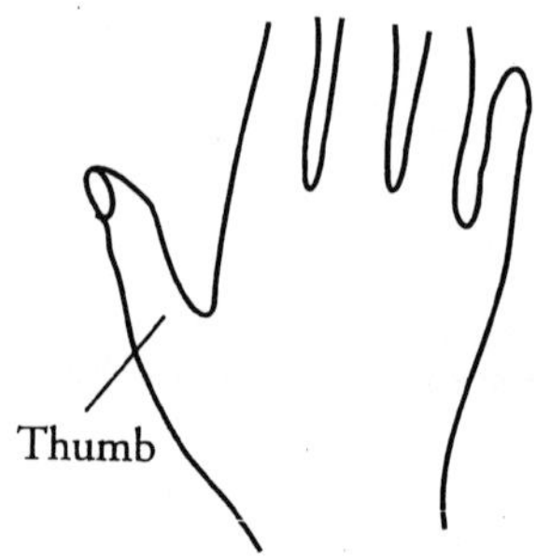

The Thumb

You can tell a lot about a person by looking at his thumb and fingers. It may come as a surprise for some but the thumb is the most important part of palm reading. It is the leading element of the hand and represents the level of life energy. On any two hands the thumbs will always be slightly different.

A thumb that holds itself close to the side of the hand shows a stingy, secretive and dishonest person.

A thumb that sticks out indicates a carefree personality.

If the thumb is set low you are very inspirational.

A high set thumb suggests a good and clearly defined instinctive creative flair.

Wide spacing between the thumb and fingers signifies generosity but a narrow spacing points to caution and restriction.

If the thumb is bulbous, then the person is prone to physical and heated tempers!

The length of the thumb should be equal to that of the little finger.

Position of the Thumb

High

This symbolises lack of adaptability, and meanness in money matters.

Low

This is a symbol of generosity.

Close to the Fingers

This is considered to be a sign of avarice (greediness & meanness).

Away from the Fingers

This indicates a spendthrift disposition.

Phalanges of the Thumb

The thumb has three phalanges.

First Phalange of the Thumb

The first phalange indicates the person's will power and levels of energy and decisiveness. It also indicates logic, while the phalange containing the nail indicates will power.

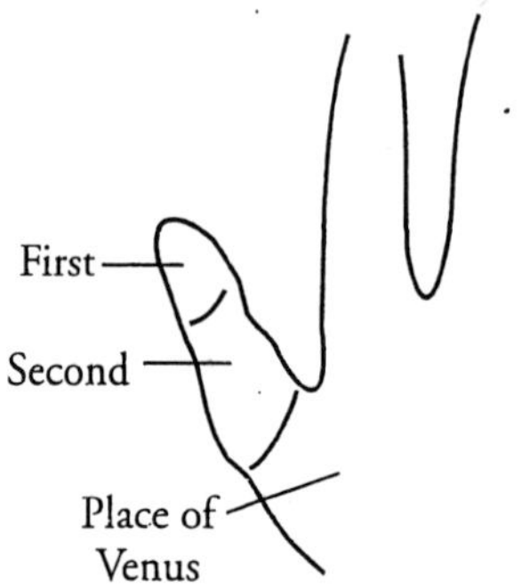

Phalanges of the Thumb

If the first phalange of the thumb is very long, then such a person is self-willed while he has less desire to work if the thumb is shorter. Such persons are weak-willed.

If the fore part of the thumb is squarish, the person is clever in legal matters and is respected for his acts of justice. A square-tipped thumb show the person to be a realist and a natural leader.

He is very obstinate if the fore part of the thumb is wide.

If the forepart of the thumb is extraordinarily long then such a person is a murderer or a dacoit or remains engrossed in anti-social activities.

Pointed or long tips indicate creativity and intelligence.

Thumbs that have an exceptionally wide top belong to aggressive people. If the top is very narrow it indicates a sign of weakness.

A thick top joint shows a person who is blunt. The tapered tip shows a subtle way of doing things.

Second Phalange of the Thumb

The second phalange is one of reason and logic. If the phalange is long, the person having it said to be efficient and strategic. They are clever and careful, and take a lead in social activities. They are held in high esteem by the society.

If the phalange is short, the person works without any forethought. He works in acts of dangerous magnitude. His perceptive powers too are poor.

If this phalange is clumsy, then he is devoid of the power of reasoning.

If this phalange is depressed then the person's mind is sharp and sensitive.

Third Part of the Thumb or Place of Venus

The ball of the thumb is called the Mount of Venus. It must be firm and springy, for it represents emotions, empathy, grace and compassion. The fatter and fleshier it is, the more sensitive and compassionate the individual.

The third part of the thumb is not a phalange, instead it the place of Venus.

Persons who have this part more prominent and elegant, and having a pink tinge, are well advanced in love matters. They gain full popularity among friends. They succeed in life and smile under adversities as well.

If the Mount of Venus protrudes very much, then the person would be sexually immoral.

If this part is less prominent or submerged with more than necessary lines on it, then the person is prone to a frustrated temperament.

If the ball of the thumb is heavier than the other areas then the physicality of the person will be strong.

A strong thumb on the left hand and a weaker one on the right denote problems as well as initiative.

If both thumbs are strong, a stubborn character is denoted, and two weak thumbs suggest a follower.

The larger the thumb, the stronger the personality, especially if it is accompanied by a strong index finger.

Different Types of Thumbs

The shape of the thumb is very important. What does your thumb shape tell you about the kind of person you are?

Long Thumb

A long thumb indicates a good leader with a determined nature; the subject is his own master.

Such persons are self-willed and self-dependent, and control others. In their lives intelligence has more importance and they are called intellectuals. They are especially interested in mathematics and engineering.

Long, broad thumbs belong to people who push hard and succeed.

Long, narrow thumbs belong to people who want to succeed but don't have the driving force.

Small, broad thumbs belong to people who lack determination.

Very Long Thumb

In such a case the head governs rather than the feelings. The person is obstinate, and not always wise.

Short Thumb

A short thumb represents an indecisive and sensitive person. A short thumb is a sign of an irresolute mind and weak reasoning.

Small thumbs indicate the persons to be gentle. They have little energy and are rather weak.

Such persons do not work with their own mind; instead they do so under the influence of others. Emotions have a more prominent place in their lives than intelligence. They take special interest in poetry, painting or music.

Broad Thumb

This is an indication of violent outbursts; if it is short as well, such persons are prone to fits (frenzy) of stubbornness that do not last long.

Hard Thumb

Such persons are obstinate and alert. They possess the capacity to keep anything to themselves. They are wanting in emotions in their lives and they mostly work on the strength of intelligence. People in possession of a stiff thumb usually display plenty of common sense, often stubbornness, exaggerated caution and secretiveness.

Flexible and Supple Thumb

A person with such a thumb is much interested in amassing wealth, and is capable of adjusting according to circumstances. This is an indication of someone who is a spendthrift, and who has unconventional tendencies.

Naturally Thrown-back Thumb

This type of thumb is an indicator of generosity and artistic talents.

Obtuse-angled thumb

If the thumb makes an obtuse angle with the index finger then it comes under this category. Such thumbs are well formed, long and thin. They are called gentle thumbs. Persons having such thumbs are gentle and sweet-tempered. They are mostly artists and musicians.

Large Thumb

A large thumb shows a strong personality. Such persons are practical and have a strong disposition.

Pointed Thumb

A pointed thumb suggests the person to be an idealist.

Thick Thumb

A thick thumb indicates primitive tastes, a rough and abrupt nature, and often uncouth ways. People with a thick thumb are also blunt and honest.

Flat Thumb

This one points towards someone with a nervous disposition.

Slender Thumb

This type of thumb belongs to those who are often artistic. It is often found in people with poetic and artistic tastes, or at least refined tastes.

Right-angled Thumb

Such a thumb forms a right angle with the index finger. These thumbs are elegant, strong and appear like pillars. Such persons believe in hard work.

They are short-tempered but quickly cool off. They stick to their words. The feeling of revenge is very strong in them.

Such persons can be neither good friends nor good enemies.

Acute-angled Thumb

A thumb that makes an acute angle at the joint with the index finger comes under this category. Such a thumb is comparatively smaller and looks clumsy, denoting an evil quality.

Persons with this kind of thumb are frustrated throughout their lives. They are very lazy and do not take the trouble to complete any work. They indulge in bad habits with lavish spending.

They are less interested in religion and are more inclined towards ghosts, spirits and the like.

They are always attracted towards the other women in life.

Club-shaped Thumb

This type indicates a tendency.

Shapes of Fingers

Heavy Fingers

These show a physical nature.

Long and Slim

Long and slim fingers signify more of an emotional and aggressive type of person.

Short and Thick Fingers

These show that the person is very emotionally comfortable.

Pointed Fingers

People with tapered, almost pointed-like fingers are cautious, intelligent and flexible. They are conversationalists and their work involves their interacting with other people.

They are interested in spiritualism and have an interest in anything new, modern and revolutionary.

Conical Fingers

These people are sensitive types. They take great care about how they look.

Conical Finger

They think quickly and have firm convictions.

They must be careful however not to let their emotions rule them.

Square Fingers

These people are business-minded, rational, practical and down-to-earth. They are also conventional, liking to stick to the norm.

Square Finger

Spatulate Fingers

These people are realistic. They prefer the outdoor life and go for adventure in life. Although most of them like travelling, yet they value work and regard it as important.

Spatulate Finger

Straight Fingers

These people are honest, sometimes too much so. They are diligent and energetic. They are great thinkers and often do well in life.

Straight Finger

Knotty Fingers

These people are extremely practical and great planners. So much so that spontaneity is a rare word with them. Their straightforward approach to life means they tend to be careful in all aspects of their life.

Knotty Finger

Finger Length

The length of the fingers provides a lot about a person's character.

A long-fingered person is analytical and academic, liking to study things in detail.

A person with markedly short fingers is very practical and intuitive, liking to go with his gut instinct.

When the hands are in proportion it shows a balanced personality. The proportion of the fingers in relation to each other is very important.

They each stand for a character marking and indicate the strength of that quality.

a) **Forefinger:** Confidence, ego, ambition, drive.

b) **Middle finger:** Discipline, balance.

c) **Ring finger:** Emotional expression, creativity.

d) **Little finger:** Communication.

A balanced ego is indicated when the forefinger reaches the bottom of the nail of the middle finger.

Balanced emotions are indicated when the ring finger reaches the bottom of the nail of the middle finger.

Great confidence is indicated when the forefinger reaches past the bottom of the nail of the middle finger.

Very emotional and creative impulses are indicated when the ring finger reaches past the bottom of the nail of the middle finger.

A lack of confidence is indicated when the forefinger doesn't reach past the bottom of the nail of the middle finger.

Blocked emotions are indicated when the ring finger doesn't reach past the bottom of the nail of the middle finger.

When the middle finger is prominent, standing out from the rest, it shows a serious and intense nature.

When the little finger stands out naturally from your hand it shows an independent and outspoken nature.

Shape of Fingertips

Square Fingertips

A full set of square fingertips in palmistry shows us an orderly and methodical type of person.

People who have these fingertips tend to be careful and methodical thinkers. They take a rational view of life. However, on the down side they tend to lack creativity.

Found often in accountants, for such people everything must be in its proper place with the highest degree of accuracy. The fingers tend to sit close together and the tips are smooth. A long middle finger will support this further. These people believe in getting ahead and succeeding in life.

Pointed Fingertips

These people have a sensitive and fragile personality. These fingertips are associated with artists, writers, poets and daydreamers.

Conical Fingertips

These people have a flexible disposition and make good negotiators. Emotional security is important for peace of mind.

Spatulate Fingertips

These are action people who tend to be dynamic thinkers.

They are usually inventors, explorers and pioneers in new industries.

It is usually found that people who like to work outdoors have spatulate fingertips. They like to be constantly on the move.

These same people often are good inventers as well.

Markings on Fingers

Signs found on fingers are of great importance to a palmist. They have great significance in criminology.

A person's character and his way of thinking can be known fully. His individuality can be understood with the help of these signs. These signs are:

Javelin

If there is a sign of a javelin or an arrow in the first phalange of the finger, then the person is very capable and learned from an intellectual point of view.

Such persons succeed in adverse condition and are capable of working according to the situation.

Such persons have heart trouble in their old age.

Tent

People with signs like a tent on the phalanges of fingers are kind-hearted and rise very high by means of their artistic talents. They also take undue advantage of others.

They are unbalanced mentally and their family life is troublesome.

Circle

A sign of a circle on fingers is considered auspicious. Such persons are independent in their thoughts and originality is seen in all they do.

They keep away from old beliefs and conservatism.

Arch

Persons with arches on their fingers are generally lazy and of suspicious nature. They do not have confidence in themselves and also in others.

They create an atmosphere of illusion around them.

They gain special success in mystic works and detective services.

Triangle

The sign of a triangle marks a man as being mysterious.

Such persons are able to make their bodies strong by practising yoga.

They love loneliness and are orthodox.

Star

Persons on whose fingers the sign of a star or a cross is visible are very fateful and fortunate. They receive wealth in life quite unexpectedly many times.

They remain happy from the financial point of view.

Net

Fingers with nets on them are indicative that the persons will meet with more obstacles and difficulties in their life. They overcome these difficulties and come unscathed by their sheer will-power.

They are less comfortable and less happy in life.

Such signs are seen in the hands of culprits and dacoits.

Rectangle

If a rectangle appears on a finger then the person is hard working.

He is prosperous and happy in life.

If more than one of the above signs is seen on the fingers of a person, then the person is entitled to the combined benefits of those signs.

The Nails

Nails are made of a substance called '**keratin**' that is a tough, dead form of protein or horn-like material.

Fingernails grow about 50 millimetres in a year.

While examining the nails, their colour and texture should not be ignored. The nails show the state of health and disposition of person.

Ancient scriptures claim that planets influence, filter into the blood through the nails, and vibrations from the atmosphere are also absorbed through them.

Long Nails

Such nails indicate a weak physique. The person is liable to suffer from chest and lung troubles.

Long

People with long, thin and brittle nails show them to have a weak physique.

If the nails are long, thin and curved, a violent disposition in love is indicated.

If they are long, thin and narrow, then the persons are timid and cowardly.

If they are long, broad and round, then a sound judgement is indicated.

Short Nails

The possessor of short nails is aggressive in approach, impulsive in speech and action.

Short

If the nails are short, flat and shell-shaped, they indicate sure signs of paralysis.

If they are short and moonless, indications are of a poor blood circulation.

If they are short and hard, then the persons have a quarrelsome disposition.

Those with short nails, and with a soft palm are inborn critics.

Broad Nails

These are broader and square at the base.

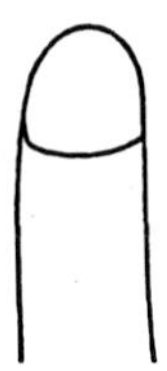

Broad

Such nails are found on square, spatulate or philosophical hands.

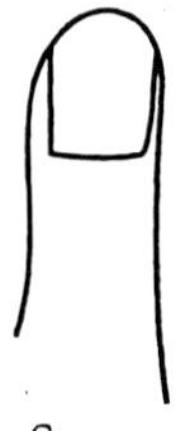

Square

They indicate good mentality, practicality, frankness, simplicity, self-confidence.

Wearing Rings on Fingers

Rings on the fingers can indicate your inner character. Wearing many rings on the hand shows the person to have an emotional armour, and relies on outer things for his well-being.

Wearing a ring on the forefinger indicates ambition, and the need to enhance one's ego.

If a person likes to wear it on the middle finger, it shows his materialistic nature.

Wearing it on the ring finger is conventional and is only noted if there are multiple or large rings adorning it. If this is the case then emotional or creative frustration could be present.

Wearing a ring on the little finger is commonly seen in the gay community. Otherwise it could indicate difficulties in sexual expression.

Fingerprints

Whorls

A person whose fingerprints are mainly whorls will be an individualistic, not just one of the crowd.

These people are often very talented and are good at keeping secrets.

Whorled fingerprints show us some artistic skills in palmistry.

Loops

Everyone gets on well with a person whose fingerprints are mainly loops.

They have good communication skills and all-round capability.

Tented Arch

These people become deeply involved in everything that they do.

Palmistry shows us much about the work directions people will take in life. People with arched fingerprints usually have jobs that are detailed special skills.

Composite Print

This is a rare print. People with this have trouble making up their mind and are difficult to deal with.

CHAPTER-8

METHODS OF SEEING HAND

Several things should be taken into consideration while studying palmistry. Some of those facts are given below for your reference.

When these rules are followed diligently, good results can be obtained from the palm-study.

1. Don't touch the hand of the person who has come for palm-analysis. This is because the vibrations in your body will come in contact with those in his body and the genuine features of his hands will be lost. Therefore keep your hands folded while seeing any hand.
2. Generally, a hand can be seen at any time, but the best time for it is morning time when the person wishing to show his hand has had neither breakfast nor taken any food. The blood circulation gets faster after food due to which the minor lines on the hand become almost invisible.
3. A person wanting his hand to be read should have bathed before showing his hand. Showing it just after sleep, with a dirty or lazy body, makes the atmosphere irrelevant and causes hindrances in foretelling.

4. A person should not show his hand after strenuous exercises or after a hard day's work as this is not favourable.
5. A hand should not be shown when it is very hot or cold outside. This is because the hand changes its colour in extreme temperature conditions.
6. No person after taking drinks or intoxicants or in sub-normal conditions should go to the palmist.
7. Also the palmist should not see any hand while he is in an angry mood or is in a perturbed state for any reason.
8. A hand should be examined in an objective manner. It is difficult for the palmist to be so if the person is a loved one or an enemy. In that case the future telling becomes more or less unrealistic.

CHAPTER-9

THE MOUNTS

Mounts are raised pads under the base of each finger and dotted around the palm. These should be soft and spongy to the touch.

Each palm has nine zones or pads more popularly known as Mounts. Each mount denotes the mental, physical, emotional peculiarities of the individual.

Mounts have a special significance in the study of palms because different lines are formed and developed there.

Mounts have been named after the planets and the special features of the planets are revealed in the corresponding mounts. It has been found that the planet more prominent in the horoscope is also prominent in the palm.

When a mount is raised and the apex is centrally located, or it has favourable signs on it, it is said to be strong.

When flat, it is ordinary, but when depressed or has bad signs on it, it is weak and unfavourable.

When a mount is overdeveloped, the qualities of the mount go to the extreme and turn adverse. For example, an underdeveloped Mount of Jupiter will make a person proud, jealous and boastful.

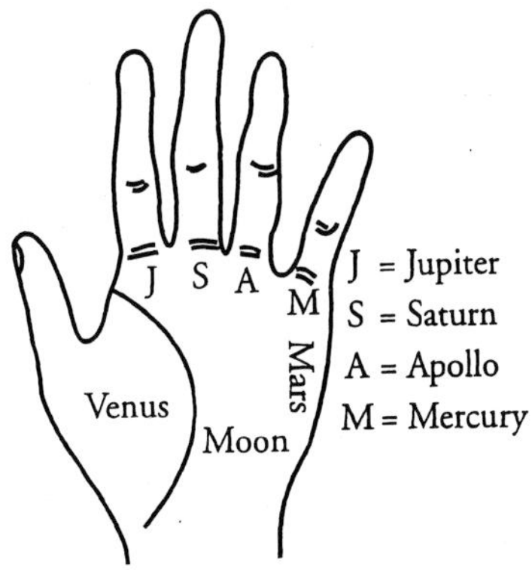

The Mounts

The different types of mounts are:

1. The Mount of Jupiter
2. The Mount of Saturn
3. The Mount of Sun or Apollo
4. The Mount of Mercury
5. The Mount of Venus
6. The Mount of Mars
7. The Mount of Luna or the Mount of Moon
8. Harshala
9. The Mount of Dragon's Head
10. The Mount of Dragon's Tail.

The names given to the mounts of the hand are associated with the seven principal planets that sway the destiny of our earth. The qualities attributed to these seven planets are:

1. Venus–Love, sensuality and passion.
2. Mars–Vitality, courage, fighting, etc.
3. Mercury–Mentality, commerce, science.
4. Moon–Imagination, romance, changeability.
5. Sun–Brilliancy, fruitfulness, success.
6. Jupiter–Ambition, power, domination.
7. Saturn–Reserve, melancholy, seriousness.

The Mount of Jupiter

The Mount of Jupiter is situated at the base of the index finger. It represents God power, leadership, self-worth, organization, ambition, religion, honour, love of nature and authority. When this is developed it reveals an ambitious nature.

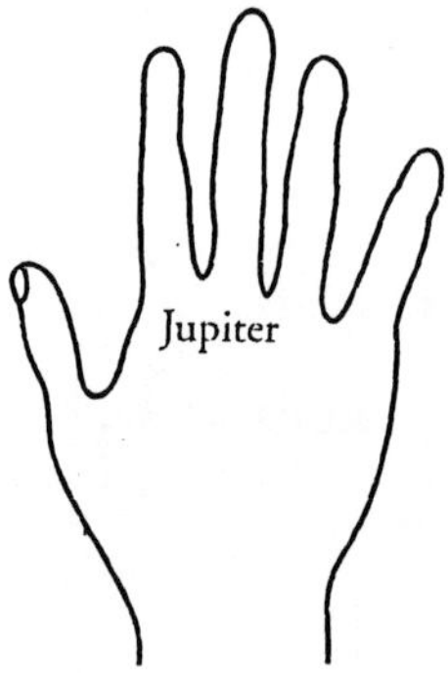

Mount of Jupiter

Persons with a well-developed Mount of Jupiter have Godly qualities. Such persons try to save their self-respect. They are learned and are always prepared to help others. They don't get disturbed under difficult conditions. All the Justices of Supreme Court and other higher courts are have a well-developed Mount of Jupiter. They have the quality to change the public in their favour. Such persons are mostly religious-minded.

If you are confident the mount will be well rounded. If it covers a wide area it shows you are generous. If it is high it suggests bossiness.

Persons with an under-developed Mount of Jupiter lack the above qualities. They have an ordinary physique but smiling faces. They are experts in delivering lectures. They are more inclined towards attainment of respect and good reputation rather than wealth. They have a soft corner for the opposite sex.

Persons with no Mount of Jupiter are found in the company of low class people and there is want of self-respect in him. They get very little patronage from their parents, and they give little respect to their parents.

Persons with an over-developed Mount of Jupiter are selfish, self-willed and proud.

The Mount of Jupiter is said to be very helpful in life and helps the person towards progress.

The Mount of Saturn

The Mount of Saturn is situated at the bottom of the middle finger. It is one of the most important mounts as it is the balance of the hand. The development of this Mount on the palm is indicative of extraordinary tendencies.

A large mount indicates a gloomy attitude.

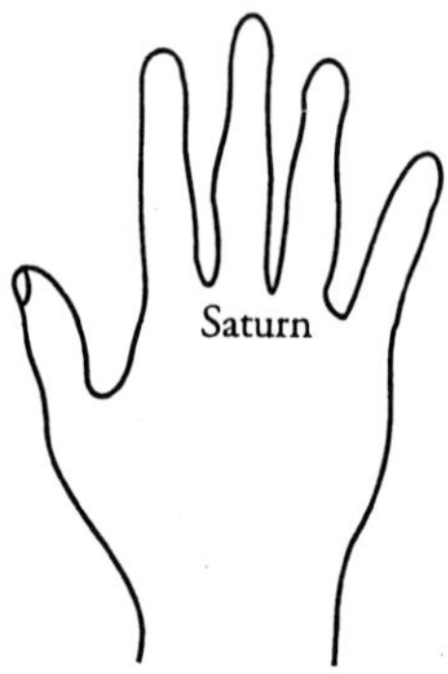

Mount of Saturn

People with a well-developed Mount of Saturn possess a good sense of responsibility and are concerned with seeking wisdom. They are highly fortunate and rise very high in life with their own efforts.

Persons with an under-developed Mount of Saturn could commit suicide in his life. This mount generally occurs in the hands of dacoits, cheats and robbers.

Persons with no Mount of Saturn have no importance in their life but they get a special kind of success or respect in life.

The Mount of Saturn represents sanity, sobriety, wisdom, introversion and karmic events such as good or bad luck.

If the Mount is fully developed then the person is highly fortunate and rises very high in life with his own efforts. But such a person likes to remain aloof and constantly moves towards his goal. He gets totally engrossed in his work, that he neglects his family. By nature they are irritating and suspicious.Persons with prominent Mount of Saturn are Wizards, Engineers, Scientists, Literary men or Chemists.

If this Mount is very much developed, then the person commits suicide in his life. This Mount is prominent in the hands of dacoits, cheats and robbers. The mount in such cases are yellowish or pale.

If there are more than necessary lines on the Mount then such a person is a coward and very licentious.

If the Mount is missing in the palm, then such a person's life has no importance. But he might get a special kind of success or respect in life. If the Mount is protruded ordinarily then the person has more than necessary faith in fate and shall succeed in his plans. Such persons have very few friends.

The Mount of Sun or Apollo

Mount of Apollo is situated at the base of the ring finger and on the upper part of the heart line. It represents self-confidence, kindness and grandeur. This mount represents the artistic side in us when it is developed and the selfish side when it is flat.

A stongly developed mount indicates an interest in the arts.

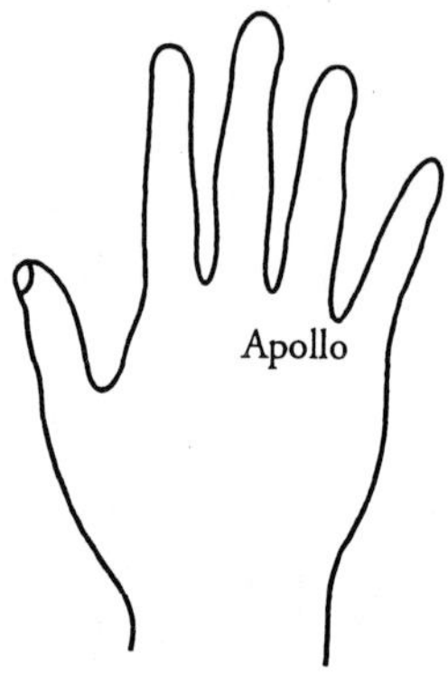

Mount of Apollo

Person with well-developed mount of Apollo becomes a genius and famous. They are of cheerful nature and work in close co-operation with friends.

Persons with under-developed mount of Apollo would be interested in beauty. But they would not be able to succeed in this field.

Persons with no mount of Apollo leads a very ordinary life. They would be a boring, dull minded and stupid fellow.

Persons with over developed mount of Apollo would be very pompous, arrogant and a flatterer. The Mount of Sun is situated at the base of the finger of Apollo and on the upper part of the heartline. This Mount is indicative of the success of the individual.

The Mount of Apollo below the ring represents confidence, creativity, impulsiveness and extroversion.

With the prominence of this Mount, the man becomes a genius and famous. A person reaches a very high status in life if the mount is well-developed and pink in colour. Such persons are of cheerful nature and work in close co-operation with friends. Such persons are successful as Artists, Expert Musicians and Painters. They are inborn genius. They are honest in their dealings and are completely materialistic. Very well developed Mount indicates self-confidence, gentlemanness, kindness and grandeur.

If the Mount is not prominent then the person would be interested in beauty. But he would not be able to succeed in this field.

If the Mount is developed more than necessary then such a person would be very proud and a flatterer. He would be having friends from the lower sections. They are extravagant and quarrelsome and never succeed in life.

If the Mount is absent, then the person leads a very ordinary life. He would be a dull-minded and foolish fellow.

The Mount of Mercury

Mount of Mercury is situated at the base of the little finger. It represents materialistic prosperity and affluence. It represents a forte in business if developed and poor communication skills if flat.

Being well-developed indicates a warm, receptive nature. Under-developed shows a loner.

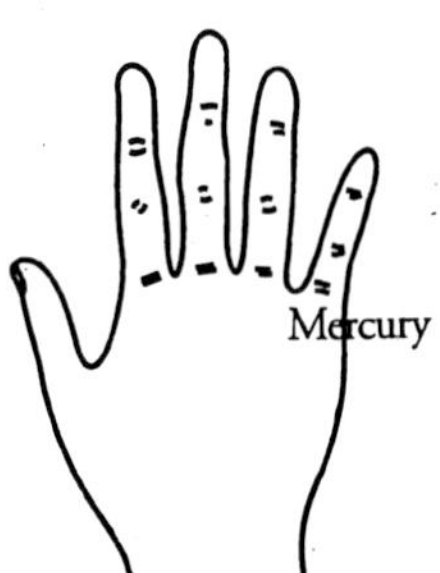

Mount of Mercury

Person with well-developed mount of Mercury would be interested in inventions and scientific works.

Persons with under-developed mount of Mercury would be a criminal of higher order. They believe in breaking the law.

Persons with no mount of Mercury live his life in poverty and lack of means.

Persons with over-developed mount of Mercury are clever and crafty and are adept in cheating.

The prominent part on the base of the finger of Mercury is called the Mount of Mercury. This Mount shows materialistic prosperity and afflunce. But much importance is not attached to this Mount of late.

The Mount of Mercury below your little finger has to do with ability to sell yourself, communication, quickness, connection as well as writing and mathematical abilities. Sometimes the Mount of Mercury will be feathered with short vertical lines that are called Lines of Affection. These sometimes indicate the number of deep emotional connections or significant relationships in a person's life.

Persons with greatly developed Mount are clever and crafty and are adept in cheating. If the Mount is ordinarily developed and has a square mark on it then such a person would be a criminal of higher order. Such persons believe in breaking the law. Persons with prominent Mount are experts in Psychology and know how to influence others. They gain success in business.

If the Mount is very much protruded then such persons are after money and the main aim of their lives is to amass wealth.

If the Mount is absent in the palm of a person then the person passes his life in poverty. If the Mount is ordinarily prominent then he would be interested in inventions and scientific works.

The Mount of Venus

Mount of Venus is situated under the thumb and surrounded by the age line. Only persons with prominent Mount of Venus can only recognize the world properly and enjoy it. If well rounded it points to a healthy libido. Family life is also important.

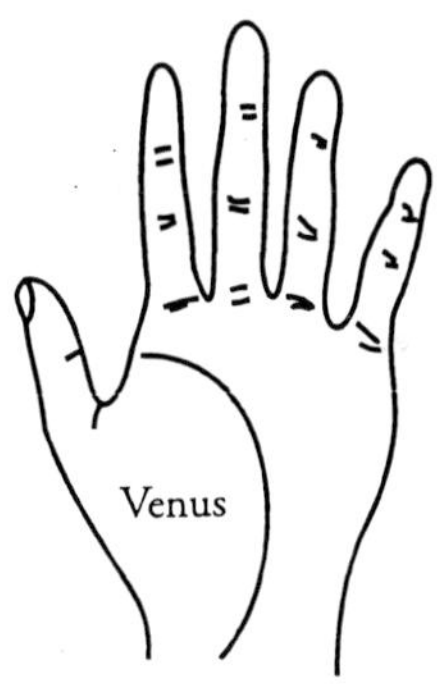

Mount of Venus

Heavily developed it shows a strong sex drive. Underdeveloped shows poor health.

Person with well-developed mount of Venus are licentious and always covet for the opposite sex. They do not have any faith in God.

Persons with under-developed mount of Venus would be a coward and weak-natured. Unloved and unwanted at home.

Persons with no mount of Venus are lives the life of an ascetic and has no interest in family life. The person's life would be full of troubles and miseries.

Persons with over-developed mount of Venus are beautiful and civilized. They are very healthy, courageous and are able of influence others. They do not lack courage.

The spot beneath the second phalange of the thumb and surrounded by the age line is called the Mount of Venus. Only persons with prominent Mount of Venus can only recognise the world properly and enjoy it.

If the Mount is less prominent in a person's hand then he would be a coward and weak-natured.

If the Mount is absent in one's hand then he lives the life of an ascetic and has no interest in family life. The person's life would be full of troubles and miseries.

The Mount of Mars

Mount of Mars is situated between the head line and beginning of the heart line. It represents war. Persons who have the Mount of Mars on their palms become courageous, fearless and frank. Those whose Mars zone is prominent have resistance to illness and bundles of energy. Those with an overdeveloped zone possess a rebellious streak.

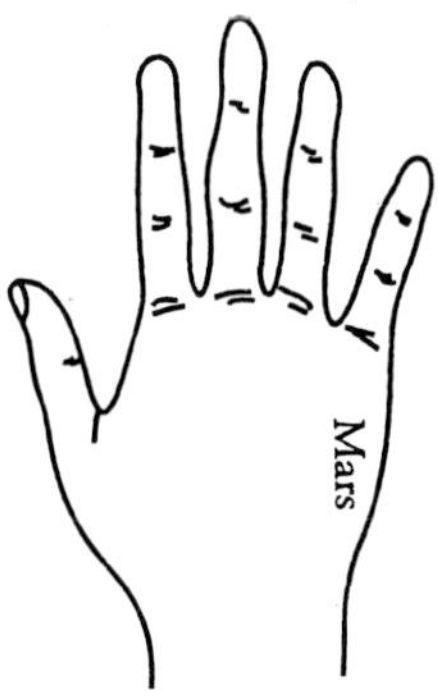

Mount of Mars

Well developed it represents courage and a fighting spirit. If it is flat it indicates a cruel streak. PLAIN OF MARS When overdeveloped it shows the person has a temper. Underdeveloped indicates a shy person.

Person with well-developed mount of Mars are courageous, fearless and powerful. They have firmness and a balance in life.

Persons with under-developed mount of Mars the person shall reach greater heights in life.

Persons with no mount of Mars can be considered as a coward.

Persons with over-developed mount of Mars then the person would be a villain, tyrant and a criminal. He would be the first in all anti-social activities.

Right below the Mount of Mercury (below the little finger) there are two more mounts. About half way down is the Mount of Upper Mars, which reflects your temperament: if this mount is fleshy then the person tends to be more courageous or war-like. Below that, near the base of the hand is the Mount of Luna (also known as the Mount of the Moon). This mount reflects such qualities as generosity, warmth and imagination. If it is over pronounced it can indicate a tendency to madness.

There are two Mars on the palm. They are known as Progressive Mars and Regressive Mars. The Surrounded portion beneath the starting point of the Lifeline and above the Mount of Venus is called the Mount of Mars. Bascially, this Mount is indicative of war. A man becomes courageous, fearless and frank by the presence of the Mount of Mars.

Below the Mount of Jupiter (follow the index finger downwards) lies the Lower Mars, which deals with aggression, hostility and capacity for evil. The centre of the palm is called the Plane of Mars. If the plane has a dip in it you are calm, cool and collected. If it is raised or flat you are more likely to display a bad temper.

Persons with prominent Mount of Mars are courageous, fearless and powerful. They are neither cowards nor can be subdued. They have a firmness and a balance in life.

If the Mount turns out to be very prominent then the person would be a villain, tyrant and a criminal. He would be the first in all anti-social activities.

If the Mount of Mars is quite developed and the palm is reddish in colour then the person shall reach greater heights in life. He gets complete success in life.

If a cross sign is found on the Mount of Mars then the person shall meet his death in war or while fighting with others. If a zig-zag line is found then the person is likely to die in an accident.

A person can be considered as a coward if the Mount of Mars is absent in his palm.

The Mount of Luna or the Mount of Moon

Mount of Moon is situated at the base of the palm, opposite the thumb. It represents imagination, beauty and emotions. If rounded and firm it points to a strong imagination and if overdeveloped, there is a lack of creativity.

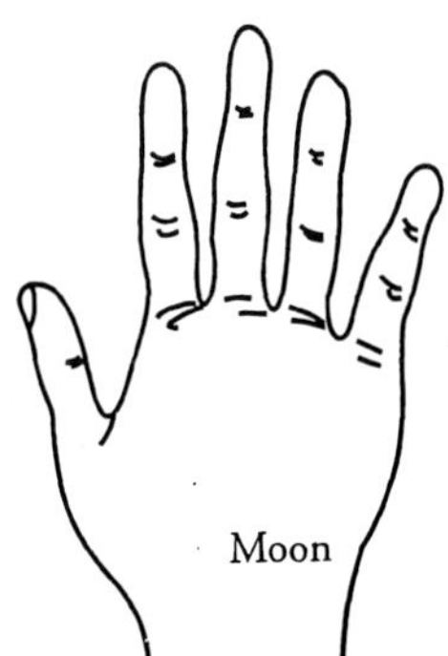

Mount of Moon

Well developed it indicates psychic ability.

Person with well-developed mount of Moon are lovers of nature and beauty. Such persons are full of religious ideas and can be artists, musicians and men of letters.

Persons with under -developed mount of Moon is imaginative and makes castles in the air. Such persons are very much emotional.

The mount of Moon is formed on the palm on the left of the lifeline and below the bracelet, also below the area of Neptune where it joins the life line. The presence of the Mount of Moon on a palm makes a man imaginative, a lover of beauty and very emotional.

Persons with fully developed Mount of Moon are lovers of nature and beauty. They remain in the dream world. There is no lack of imagination in their lives. Such persons are high class Artists, Musicians and Men of Letters. They are full of religious ideas.

If the Mount is fairly developed then the person is imaginative and makes castles in the air. He makes many plans but none of them are completed, some not even started. They are too emotional.

Persons not having the Mount of Moon are hard-hearted and fully materialistic. They have fighting as their main trait.

If zig-zag lines are found on this Mount then the person shall go on voyages several times in life. If a circle is found on the Mount, then such a person shall go to foreign countires for political reasons.

If this Mount is more than developed, then that person is found to be fickle-minded, suspicious or mad. He suffers from headache all the time.

Harshala

This planet is more powerful and exerts more influence in comparison with the other planets. It has its area of influence on the palm between the Heart and the Head lines. Its area is a little below the little finger and the Mount of Mercury. This planet influences the heart and the brain. A man having this Mount below the Mount of Mercury and between the heart and the head lines becomes a world-famous Scientist or Mathermatician. They become successful dealing with atoms, televisions and other intricate items.

If this Mount is less prominent then such a person takes interest in the works connected with machines. He becomes famous throughout the world if a line comes from Harshal and goes towards the fingers of Apollo.

The Mount of Neptune

The area of this planet on the palm is below the head line and above the Mount of Moon. A man becomes an eminent Musician, Poet or Writer if this Mount is very prominent. If a line is seen on this Mount and this line meets the fate line a little ahead, the person gets some post of great importance. If developed, this reflects a deep understanding of people.

If it is well-developed it shows a charismatic person.

If this Mount is develpepd more than enough then such a person's life would be full of grief and his family life would be spoilt. They are maniacs, suspicious and cruel.

The Mount of Pluto

Its area on the palm is below the heart line and above then head line and is situated between the Mounts of Harshal and Jupiter. This Mount can be clearly seen on the hand of every person. When this is well-developed there is an interest in the occult.

Its influence can be seen only in the old age. If this Mount is very prominent, then the person passes his old age happily. If a cross sign is found on this Mount, the person will die before the age of 45 in an accident.

If the Mount is too prominent then the person would be rude, illiterate and prodigal and has to face many difficulties in life. He would not get any co-operation from his family and friends.

If the Mount is not prominent then the person would be unlucky. His nature turns irritable and troublesome.

The Mount of Dragon's Head

Its area is situated below the headline, surrounded by the Mounts of Moon, Mars and Venus. The fate line passes over this Mount while going towards the Mount of Saturn.

If the Mount is prominent and protruded then the person would be very fortunate. If the fate line is deep and clear while passing over the prominent Mount of Pluto then he would be a genius, religious-minded and shall enjoy all wordly comforts. If the Mount is prominent and the fate line is broken then the person shall get wealthy suddenly and also fall down suddenly in life.

If the Mount is less protruded then the person would be a restless character and will lose all his wealth.

The Mount of Dragon's Tail

The place of this Mount is a little above the bracelets, dividing the Mounts of Venus and Moon and is near the starting point of the fate line. This planet shows its influence from the 5th year to the 20th year of age. If the Mount is ordinarily prominent and protruded and the fate line is deep and clear, the person would be fortunate and shall enjoy all pleasures in his lifetime. If the Mount is unusually protruded and the fate line is weak then he has to experience hardships in his young age. The financial position of his family also gets worser day by day.

A man can advance in life only when the Mount of Dragon's Tail is prominent and the fate line is clear and prominent.

Markings on the Mounts

Mount of Apollo

1. A star on the mount of Apollo is a very good sign that indicates wealth and prestige.
2. A triangle on the Mount of Apollo indicates good luck.

3. A cross is not a good sign and may indicate the failure of dreams.
4. A circle is very rare and indicates fame.

Lower Mount of Mars

1. A cross on the Lower Mount of Mars protects against a risk of sudden death.
2. A grille indicates someone with a argumentive nature.
3. A triangle will indicate fame will come from a brave deed.
4. A star shows someone who will achieve their goals through their own hard work.

Upper Mount of Mars

1. A cross on the upper Mount of Mars shows a person who will never forgive an injustice.
2. It also indicates a person who tends to argue a lot.
3. A star on the upper Mount indicates this person may have a violent nature.
4. A triangle shows a person with a high level of courage. These people also tend to do well in a military career.
5. A square on the upper Mount of Mars is a good sign of protection.
6. However a grile is a bad sign that may indicate a violent death.

Mount of Mercury

1. A star on the Mount of Mercury indicates a successful professional career.
2. A cross under the Mount will protect your job or business against any bad luck.

3. A cross on the mount indicates diplomacy.
4. A square on the Mount of Mercury indicates someone who would be a good teacher.
5. A triangle shows someone who gets on well with other people.
6. A grill is not a good sign and indicates nervous problems.

Mount of Moon

1. A star on the Mount of the Moon shows someone who has a very vivid imagination.
2. A circle on the Mount indicates a warning against travel on water.
3. A cross indicates someone who tends to have exaggerated views in life.
4. A square will give you protection against danger in travel.
5. A grille is a bad sign and may indicate illness.

Mount of Neptune

1. A circle, star, or triangle on the Mount of Neptune indicates great artistic and musical talent.
2. However, a cross or grille is not a good sign. It indicates someone who may have problems with drugs or alcohol.

Mount of Pluto

1. A triangle on the mount of Pluto adds to your powers in the occult.
2. A grille indicates strong psychic powers.
3. A line of intuition indicates a true psychic.

Mount of Venus

1. A cross on the Mount of Venus indicates the person will find true love in his life.
2. A triangle on the Mount of Venus shows a person who will marry for money.
3. A star at the base of the Mount of Venus indicates trouble in finding true love in life.
4. A grill on the Mount of Venus is a sign of sensuality.
5. A island on the Mount of Venus indicates a loss of opportunities.
6. Small circles on the Mount will indicate adultery.
7. A square will act as protection in love.

CHAPTER-10

THE LINES

An interesting question often heard in palmistry is, why do some people have many lines but others only a few ? Well, first you will notice that mostly men tend to have fewer lines than women. When one sees the palm one will notice many lines on it. These are lines of the hand. These lines can be many, like the Head Line, Heart Line, Life Line, Fate Line, etc.

The seven main lines are:

1. The Life Line
2. The Head Line
3. The Heart Line
4. The Line of Apollo or Sun
5. The Fate Line
6. The Health Line
7. The Marriage Line

The 12 secondary lines are:

1. The Ring of Jupiter
2. The Line of Mars
3. The Ring of Saturn
4. The Ring of Sun

5. The Girdle of Venus
6. The Moon Line
7. The Line of Influence
8. The Travel Line
9. The Lines of Children
10. The Bracelets
11. The Casual Lines
12. The High Post Line

Let us deal with each line in detail.

Below is also listed which way you read a line. For example, the Head Line is read from the end nearest the thumb, and if you laid a time line over that you would gradually increase the time and therefore the age of the person's line you are reading.

The Life Line

The Life Line is also called the "Paternal Line or Age Line". This has the greatest importance on a palm. Everything in life is in the line.

This line is read downwards towards the wrist.

The Line of Life is the most important and controversial line on hand. This line extends from the edge of the palm above the thumb and travels in an arc towards the wrist. The line, rising under the Mount of Jupiter, goes down the hand and embraces the Mount of Venus.

This line is believed to represent the person's vitality and vigour, physical health and general well-being.

This line indicates major life events as well as the health of the subject. It does not indicate how old you will live to be. What the line reveals is the quality of your life. It is an index of how much vitality, strength and energy you have. The longer this line is, the longer the individual will live.

If the Line of Life is semi-circular, thin and deep, without irregularities, breaks, or crosses of any kind, it is an auspicious sign and promises long life, good health, and vitality.

A thick, shallow and straight Line of Life is not auspicious.

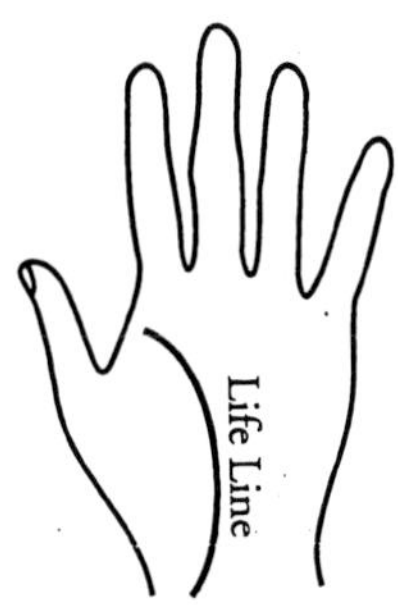

Life Line

If your Life Line is long and clear, you have good health and vitality. You approach each day with all the enthusiasm it deserves.

A short and faint line means that you lack energy and may be somewhat frail: time to recharge your batteries!

Breaks in the line show many changes in the direction of life. If you have a break in only one hand, this shows an illness followed by a speedy recovery in both hands in the same area shows a slightly more serious illness.

If your Life Line ends in a fork, this indicates long distance travel. Two small branches mean money.

A Life Line running close to the thumb indicates a person of low vitality. It is sometimes found in the hands of people who suffer from chronic fatigue syndrome.

If the Head Line is stronger than the Life Line it shows a person who is more mentally active than physically active.

A chained Life Line indicates a delicate health. Little lines rising from it indicate an active personality.

Outward swinging lines indicate a love of travel. Most of the small lines on the Life Line refer to particular events at certain times of your life.

A branch leading to the Mount of Jupiter is a sign of academic achievement. A branch that leads to the Mount of Saturn indicates a successful property transaction.

A branch towards the Mount of Apollo indicates monetary gain.

A branch towards the Mount of Mercury indicates business success.

Some of the variations of the Life Line and its representations are discussed below.

1. A perfect line, without breaks, crosses, or irregularities of any kind, promises healthy and extremely long life.
2. An imperfect line made up of little pieces like a chain or found splitting into little hair lines, represents bad health.

3. When the line starting slopes downward from the mount of Jupiter then it denotes an ambitious life.
4. A line connected with that of the head is a good sign denoting caution, carefulness.
5. All lines that rise upward from the line of life towards the mount of Jupiter show that all ambitions of the subject are fulfilled. A line rising from the life line evolving on the mount of Saturn shows a golden period of life. A line from the life to the mount of the Sun indicates glory and success due to the subject's own life, and not to outside circumstances or to chances.
6. Lines running in the opposite direction cutting the line of life show worries and obstacles.
7. When the lines of life, head, and heart are all joined together at the commencement, it is a very unfortunate sign, denoting that the person has bad temperament and he may put himself in danger while dealing with other people.
8. A medium space between head and life line denotes that the subject is more free to carry out the plans of the life and have great energy and self-confidence.

The Head Line

This line starts from the Mount of Jupiter or from above it. In most of the palms, the Head Line and the Life Line originate from the same place. It divides the palm into two parts.

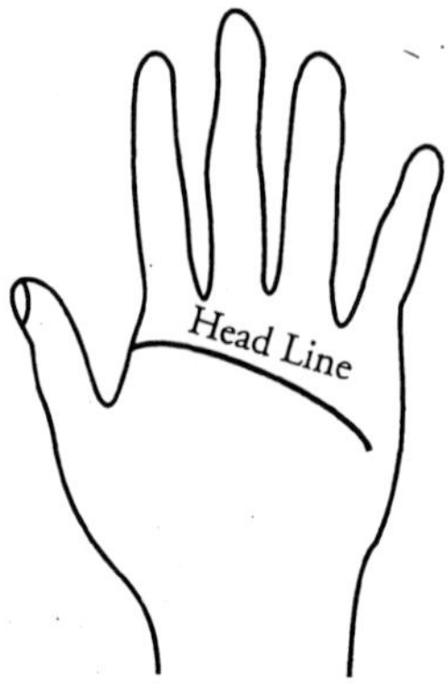

Head Line

This line starts at the edge of the palm under the index finger and flows across the palm towards the outside edge. Often, it is joined with the Life Line at inception.

The Line of Head is one of the most important lines of one's hand.

The Head Line is normally positioned and can cut across the palm or curve downward. It is an indicator of intelligence and mental health. An optimum Head Line runs straight, is deep and has a long extension almost to the other side of the palm. The more the headline curves downward towards the wrist, the less control the individual may have over his or her emotions.

This line is read from the end nearest the thumb.

The Head Line deals with your intellect, creativity and the way you handle life. This line represents your mind and the way it works, including learning style, communication style, intellectualism, and thirst for knowledge. It indicates the preference for reactive or analytical approaches to information. It also indicates your wealth.

The length of the line indicates the level of intelligence. If your line goes straight across your palm, you are a practical and down-to-earth person.

A Head Line curving toward the Heart Line indicates good business ability.

A clear and distinct Head Line shows good concentration, and if the line ends with a fork you are clever and diplomatic.

The Line of Head relates principally to the mentality of the subject to the intellectual strength or weakness, to the temperament in its relation to talent, and to the direction and quality of the talent itself. It is indicative of the mental level or the intelligence of a person. Whether a person would have money or not is also divined from a study of this line. If one goes a little deeper into things one finds that intelligence or a person's mental level has something to do with whether he would have money or not. If a person loses the capacity to act intelligently, he is sure to lose whatever money he has and, conversely, using one's wits fully can lead to affluence.

If the line is long, deep and distinct, then the person would have a sharp mind and would be an intellectual.

If it is faint, indistinct or appears broken at several places then the person would be weak-minded or a labourer.

Although the Head Line shows how a person thinks it does not show how intelligent you are. An average Head Line ends somewhere under the ring finger.

A short Head Line indicates a person whose thinking is simple and straight to the point. A long Head Line indicates a person who over things very carefully.

A straight Head Line indicates clear, concentrated thinking. A curved Head Line belongs to a person who likes to play with new ideas.

Sloping Head Lines belong to creative people. Horizontal Head Lines belong to people who look at the practical side of the matter.

Chained Head Lines belong to highly-strung people. A fork in the headline shows the ability to see more than one point of view.

A floating Head Line is indicative of someone with a carefree attitude. A Head Line that starts under the index finger indicates a brilliant mind.

Some of variations of lifeline and its representations are discussed below.

1. A Head Line that rises from the Jupiter, represents people with great brain power, ambition, and power.
2. If it rises from the Line of Life it indicates people who are very cautious and extremely sensitive.

3. If it rises inside the Life Line on the Mount of Mars it is an unfavourable sign–it indicates a frightful, worrying nature, a conflicting and quarrelling attitude.
4. A straight and clear Head Line denotes practical common sense and a love for material things more than those of the imaginations.
5. When straight in the first half, then slightly sloping, it shows a balance between the purely imaginative and the purely practical.
6. A sloping Head Line represents romance, idealism, imaginative work, and Bohemianism. When sloping and terminating with a fine fork on the Mount of Luna, it promises literary talent of the imaginative order.
7. If it is extremely long and straight, and going directly to the side of the hand (the percussion), it represents high intellectual power and selfish nature.

The Heart Line

This line starts from under the Mount of Mercury, separating the areas of Mercury and Harshala, reaching under the index finger and the Mount of Jupiter. It is the horizontal line above the Head Line. It is found towards the top of the palm, under the fingers.

This line is directly linked to the heart and is found in almost all palms.

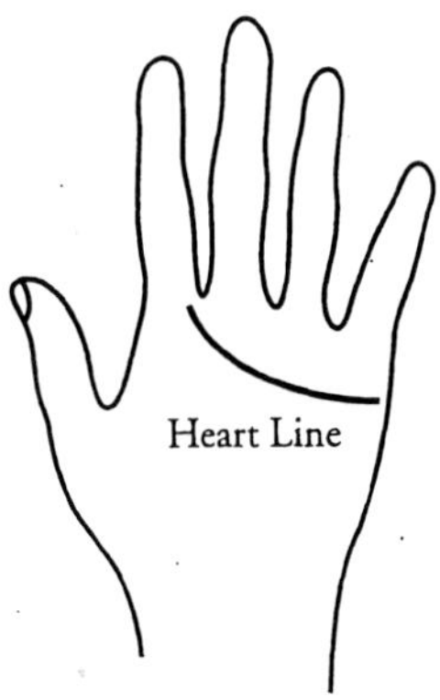

Heart Line

It represents the matters of the heart, both physical and metaphorical. It is believed to be line of emotions. It represents the attraction of the sexes from natural causes.

This line is read from the end nearest the little finger.

The line of heart should be deep, clear, and well coloured.

If your Heart Line is long and curved with some distance from the fingers, this shows a warm-hearted, kind person.

If it is longer and stronger than that of your Head Line, this means that your heart rules your head or all your decisions are emotionally based.

A very deep Heart Line and one that runs close to the fingers shows tendencies to be possessive and if you have chains on it, you could be a little bit of a flirt.

This line is absent in robbers and cruel people.

If the line is weak, then the person would be inhuman or merciless.

Imagine two heart lines extending from the edge of the hand below the little finger to between the first and second fingers. The first line is a deep curve while the second heart line is straighter. The curved line is active in romantic matters while the straight line is passive. The curved Heart Line is aggressive in love, while the straight line is receptive. The curved line is demonstrative while the straight line thinks about it. Interestingly the curved line is much more common on male hands while the straight line is more common on female hands.

If the Heart Line ends up under the index finger it indicates someone who is choosy about his partner.

It has been found that in cases where the marriage is a success the partners tend to have similar Heart Lines.

It is rare for the Heart Line to end up under the middle finger. People with this line tend to be dominated by the need for love.

When the Heart Line is straight and short, these people have no romance, only just a crude sex drive. People with a straight heart line ending on the mount of Jupiter tend to make good welfare workers. These people tend to drop out of society and go live on a commune.

Two or more branches on the Heart Line indicate a corresponding number of different sides to the emotional nature. A line that has a strong branch that reaches down and touches the Life Line indicates someone who is easily hurt in love.

Loops, chains, cuts and breaks in this line indicate relationships and episodes occurring in a person's love life.

Some of variations of the Heart Line and its representations are discussed below.

1. A heart line that rises between the first and the second fingers is the most favourable sign on the hands of a person. This sign represents a calm temperament in matters of the heart. Such persons are quieter and more subdued in their passions.

2. A line that rises from the centre of Jupiter gives the highest type of love — the pride and worship of the heart's ideal. A man possessing such a line is strong, and reliable in his affections. He believes that the woman of his choice would be great, noble and famous. Such a man has far less love affairs than the man with the line from Saturn.
3. A Heart Line that rises from the Mount of Saturn represents more passion. Such a person is less expressive as compared to those with a line from Jupiter. When such a line rises very high on the mount then such a person is far more passionate and sensual than any of the others.
4. When the line forks, with one branch resting on Jupiter, the other between the first and second fingers, it is a sign of a happy, calm nature, good fortune, and happiness in affection. But when the fork is so wide that one branch rests on Jupiter, the other on Saturn, it then denotes a very uncertain disposition, and such a person doesn't intend to make the marital relations happy because of his temperament.

The Line of Apollo or Sun

The Line of Apollo or Sun is also called the Line of Success or the Line of Brilliance. The source of the line is different in different palms but ultimately it ends at the Mount of Sun.

The line is not present in every hand but when it is, it is a sign of happiness and achievement.

The Line of Apollo is a vertical line that is found on the upper part of the Mount of the Moon. It runs parallel to the Fate Line, under the ring finger.

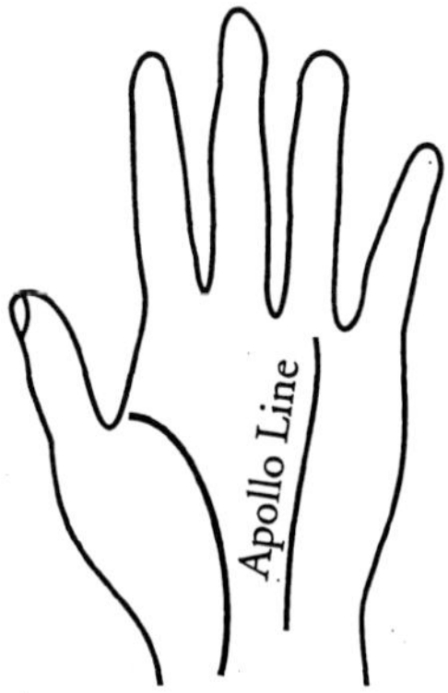

Apollo Line

It indicates fame or scandal. It increases the success given by a good Fate Line. It gives fame and distinction to the life when it is in accordance with the work and career given by the other lines in the hand.

The Apollo Line is more heavily marked on the philosophic, conic, and spatulate kinds of hands. It increases the success given by a good Fate Line, and gives fame and distinction to the life when it is in accordance with the work and career given by the other lines in the hand; otherwise it merely relates to a temperament that is keenly alive to the artistic, but unless the rest of the hand bears this out, the subject will have the appreciation of art without the power of expression.

The line has been ascribed the gift of great artistic talents, wealth and fame. It deals with your happiness and enjoyment of life.

This line is read upwards.

A clear and straight Apollo Line shows a lucky person. If the line starts from your Life Line or Fate Line you will have many successes as a result of using your talents. If it starts from your Head Line your success will come to you during your middle ages.

If the line is absent, this does not mean that the person will be unsuccessful with money. A financially secure person without a Line of Apollo will normally have a well defined Line of Fate. A Line of Apollo is more closely associated with contentment, and for some, contentment comes when material happiness does. In hands where there is no Apollo Line it tends to show that the person feels that happiness is out of reach. When there is multiple Apollo lines it may indicate a person has many talents but is master of none.

The Apollo Line is also associated with a creative talent. The line may commence from different points in the palm.

Success tends to come to those whose Apollo Line starts high in the palm. If the line is patchy it indicates that success will be patchy.

If the Apollo Line springs from the Fate Line it shows the point in life when the person's talents are recognised.

A star on the Apollo Line indicates that the person will win or come into a substantial lot of money.

An island on the Apollo Line indicates a period where there is a loss of self-esteem.

Some of variations of the Apollo Line and its representations are discussed below.

1. An Apollo Line rising from the Line of Life denotes that life will be devoted to the worship of the beautiful things.
2. A line rising from the Line of Fate increases the success promised by the Line of Fate.
3. A line rising from the Mount of Luna promises success and distinction, largely dependent upon the fancies and the help of others.
4. A line with a sloping Line of Head indicates success in poetry, literature, and things of the purely imaginative order.
5. A line rising upon the Plain of Mars promises success after difficulty.
6. A line rising from the Line of Heart denotes a great taste for art and artistic things.
7. A good Fate Line and an Apollo Line parallel to one another with a straight Line of Head is one of the greatest signs of the acquisition of wealth.

The Fate Line

The fourth main line on the palm is called the Line of Fate also known as the Line of Faith, or Line of Destiny or Saturnian Line.

This line is not visible in many hands. It is found in only 50 per cent of the population of the world.

This line runs vertically from the middle of the base of the palm and up towards the middle finger. In other words, it is located in the centre of the palm of the hand as an upright line. It commences from different places but it ends only at the Mount of Saturn. This line develops from below the palm towards the upper side.

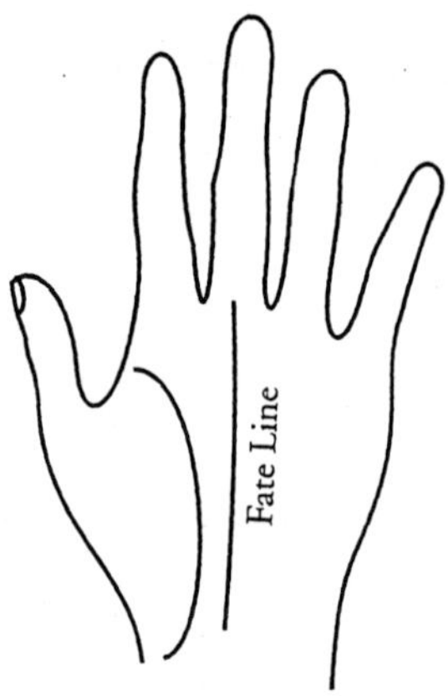

Fate Line

This line indicates the person's life path, including school and career choices, successes and obstacles, and ethics. It also reflects the circumstances beyond the individual's control, or the person's choices and their consequences. It is an indicator of material and financial strength. The deeper, stronger and less broken the line, the more likely the person is likely to be successful. It also indicates a serious, business-like nature.

In the reading of this line the type of hand plays an important part; for instance, the Line of Fate, even in the most successful hand, is less marked on the elementary, the square, and the spatulate, than on the philosophic, the conic, or the psychic. Consequently, if one sees, as one often will, an apparently very strong Line of Fate on a conic hand, one must remember that it has not half the importance of a similar line on a square type as far as worldly success is concerned. This line is read upwards.

If your Fate Line is straight and unbroken this means a successful, untroubled life. If it breaks this indicates sudden changes. We are the accumulation of our life experiences; we always need the *downs* to help us appreciate just how wonderful the *ups* are. If your Fate Line starts from the Head Line or Heart Line, this indicates success late in life, usually by your own hand.

Strong fate lines belong to people who settle into a pattern of life early. Weak fate lines tend to belong to people who are unsettled and tend to change jobs a lot.

Fate lines starting at the very bottom of the palm indicate people who settle into their life path early. When the fate line ends at the head line it indicates a person who seems to lose their way somewhere between 30 to 40 years old.

You will find that most Fate Lines end at the Heart Line. However, if it runs all the way almost to the middle finger these people tend to be active right up into old age.

A Fate Line that is tied to the heart line indicates a restricted childhood. Two Fate Lines are found on people who pursue two careers at the same time.

The absence of a Fate Line indicates a person who lacks stability. It is also found on the hands of alcoholics and drug addicts.

Some of variations of the Fate Line and its representations are discussed below.

1. If the Fate Line rises from the Line of Life and from that point on is strong, success and riches will be won by personal merit. But if the line is marked low down near the wrist and tied down, as it were, by the side of the Life Line, it tells that the early part of the person's life will be sacrificed to the wishes of parents or relatives.
2. A Line of Fate starting from the wrist and going straight and clear to its termination on Saturn denotes a strong personality. It is a sign of extreme good fortune and success.
3. If the line rises from the Mount of Luna, it denotes uncertainty in success. Fate and success will be more or less dependent on the fancy and caprice of other people. This is very often found in the case of public favourites.
4. If the line rises from a well-marked Line of Head, then success will be won late in life, after a hard struggle and through the person's talents just after 35 years.
5. If the line terminates by crossing its own Mount and goes to that of Jupiter, success will be great and satisfactory.

6. When there is a break in the line, it is a sure sign of misfortune and loss.
7. A double or sister Fate Line is an excellent sign. It denotes a distinguished career.
8. When the line rises with one branch from the base of Luna, the other from Venus, the person's destiny will sway between imagination on the one hand, and love and passion on the other.
9. If the line sends off-shoots or lines towards any other mounts but that of Saturn, it denotes that the qualities of that particular Mount will dominate the life.

The Health Line

The Line of Mercury has been variously called the Line of Health or the Line of Liver.

It is found either on Mount of Mercury or the Plain of Mars. It has no fixed place of commencement. But it terminates at the Mount of Mercury.

If there is no line you are probably blessed with excellent health. Strong markings in this area indicate troubles with health.

If the line begins on the Mount of Luna or branches from the Life Line it is a sign of a good business head.

Health and sickness are studied with the help of this line. In some cases the line is thick while in some others it is very thin like a hair.

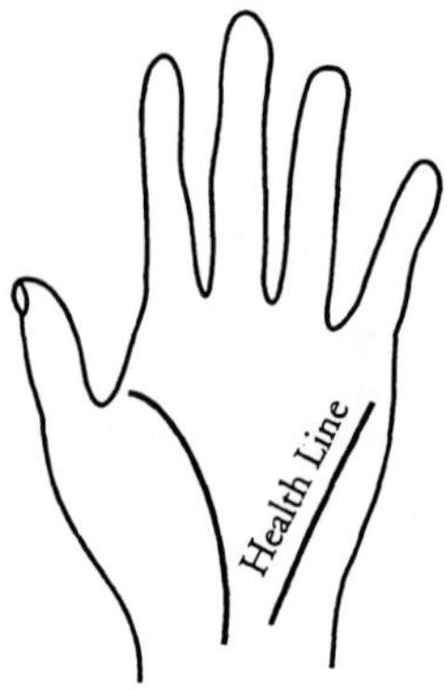

Health Line

This line foreshadows the growth of the illness or germ of disease which at the time of its coming in contact with the Line of Life will reach its climax.

It should be straight down the hand–the straighter the better, although it is an excellent sign to be without this line. Such absence denotes an extremely robust, healthy constitution. Its presence on a hand in any form indicates some delicate point to be guarded against.

Some of variations of this line and its representations are discussed below.

1. The less the length of the Line of Health, the better for the person. When it is completely absent the constitution is stronger.
2. The heavier the line the more the nervous system is impaired. When twisted and irregular, it shows biliousness, liver complaints and kidney trouble.

3. A line that is heavily marked from the heart to the head, and red in colour denotes danger of apoplexy, brain fever.
4. A line crossing the hand and touching the Line of Life at any point, represents a delicate body and a weak constitution.
5. A line formed in little straight pieces denotes bad digestion.
6. A health line in little islands, with long, filbert nails, denotes trouble to the lungs and chest.
7. When rising from the Line of Heart at the Mount of Mercury and running into or through the Line of Life, it foretells some weakness of the heart. If very pale in colour, and broad, it indicates bad blood circulation. If red in colour, particularly when it leaves the Line of Heart, it is an indication of heart trouble.

The Marriage Line

The Marriage Line is also called the Love Line.

It is situated on the Mount of Mercury. This line comes from the outside of the palm towards the inside of the palm on the Mount of Mercury. The line or lines may rise on the side of the hand or be only marked across the front of the Mount of Mercury.

In some hands three or four lines are found which does not mean that they will marry that many times.

If there is a cross on the line then the marriage or the engagement of the person would be broken.

If there are some small signs on the line then the person will have illicit affairs.

Marriage Line

From a marriage point of view, the line on the Mount of Mercury gives a very fair idea of the age at the time of marriage.

Some of variations of the line and its representations are discussed below.

1. When the Marriage Line lies close to the Line of Heart, the union will be early, in the age period of fourteen to twenty.
2. When it is near the centre of the mount, then indications are of marriage at about the age of twenty-one or twenty-eight.
3. When it is three-quarters up the mount, then marriage can take place when the person is twenty-eight to thirty-five and so on.

The Ring of Jupiter

The Ring of Jupiter makes a half moon on the Mount of Jupiter and covers its whole area which looks like a ring.

The Line of Mars

This line commences from the base of the Life Line near the thumb, passes over the area of Mars and goes towards the Mount of Venus and Line of Mars, but its place of commencement is not sure.

The Mars Line runs between the thumb and the Life Line.

The line indicates extra vitality and a sort of second protection.

The Ring of Saturn

This line surrounds the Mount of Saturn in the base finger of Saturn. Its one end lies between the finger of Saturn and the index finger, and the other end lies between the finger of Saturn and the finger of Apollo.

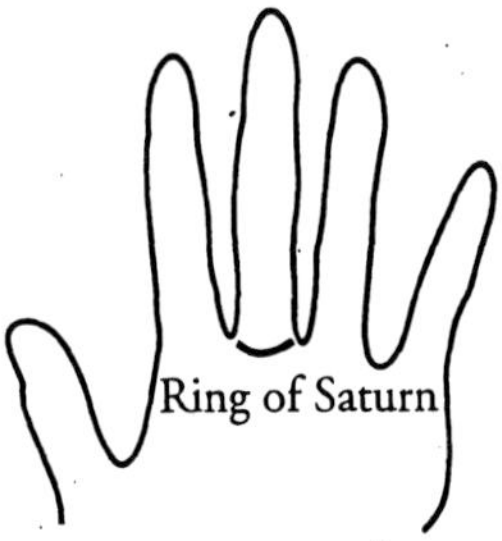

Ring of Saturn

This line is a small arc under the middle finger.

It is also another rare line.

People with this line are often referred to as boring.

The Ring of Apollo

This surrounds the Mount of Sun or Apollo like a ring. One end of the ring lies between the finger of Saturn and the finger of Apollo, and the other end lies between the finger of Apollo and the little finger. The shape of the ring remains the same in all hands.

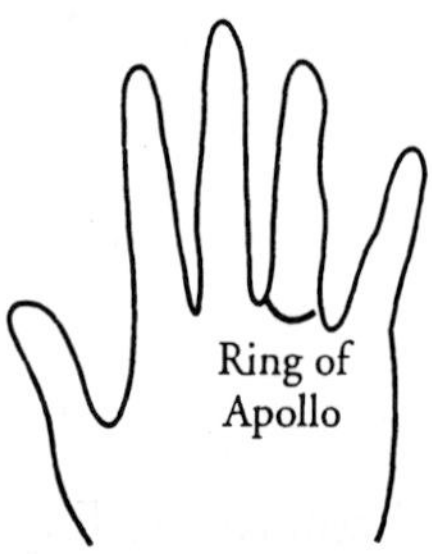

Ring of Apollo

The Girdle of Venus

There are many minor lines that don't appear in every hand but one of the best known is the Girdle of Venus that starts between the Mounts of Jupiter and Saturn and ends around the little finger. It encircles both the Mounts of Sun and Saturn.

In other words, it is a kind of semicircle rising between the first and second fingers and finishing between the third and fourth.

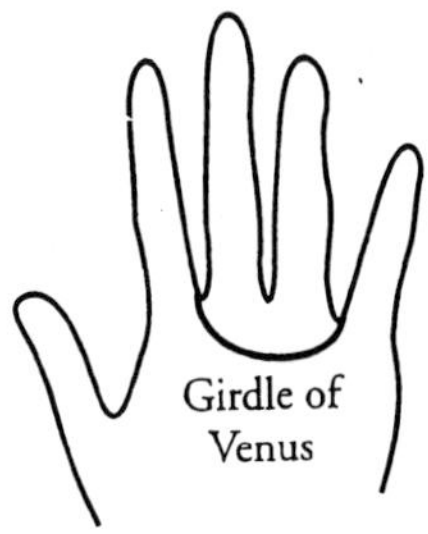

Girdle of Venus

This line looks like a loop circling three of your four fingers, and its presence is supposed to indicate beauty and luck in romance. The hand is filled with all kinds of markings, lines, feathers, stars, and crosses—each with particular meanings.

Despite the name it has no connection with the Mount of Venus.

This mark denotes highly sensitive intellectual natures, but natures changeable in moods, easily offended, and touchy over little things. It relates to emotional intelligence and the ability to manipulate. It denotes a highly-strung, nervous temperament, and when unbroken, it certainly gives a most unhappy tendency towards hysteria and despondent.

Some of variations of this line and its representations are discussed below.

1. People possessing the Girdle of Venus are capable of rising to the highest pitch of enthusiasm over anything that engages their fancy, but keep on fluctuating between high and low spirits.

2. When the girdle goes over the side of the hand and comes in contact with the line of marriage, the happiness of the marriage will be marked through the peculiarities of the temperament. Such people are peculiarly exciting, and hard to live with. If it is present on a man's hand, that man would want as many virtues in a wife as there are stars in the universe.

The Moon Line

This is a line in the shape of a bow. It commences from the area of the Moon, passes over the Neptune and Harshala areas and ends after reaching the Mount of Mercury. This line is seen in very few hands.

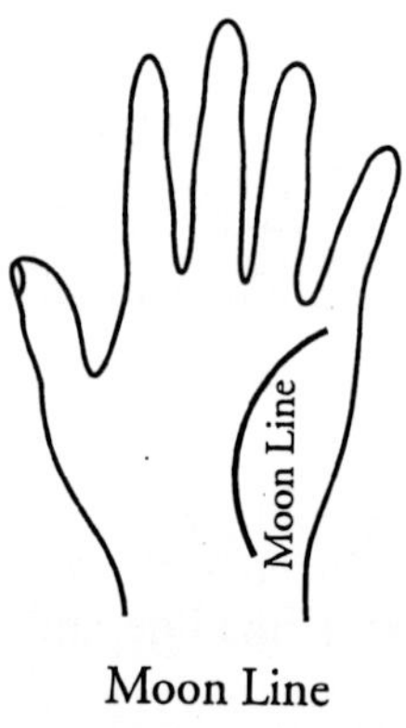

Moon Line

The Line of Influence

This line enhances the influence of any line with which it is found.

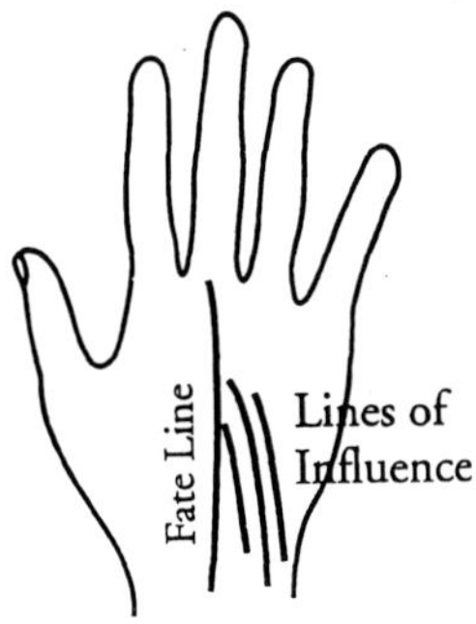

Lines of Influence

This line passes over the areas of Moon and Neptune and reaches the Fate Line. In some hands it is double and in some hands it is treble. Its origin is from the Mount of Venus.

The Travel Line

Is our desire to travel written in our palm already? What does the travel line mean for you?

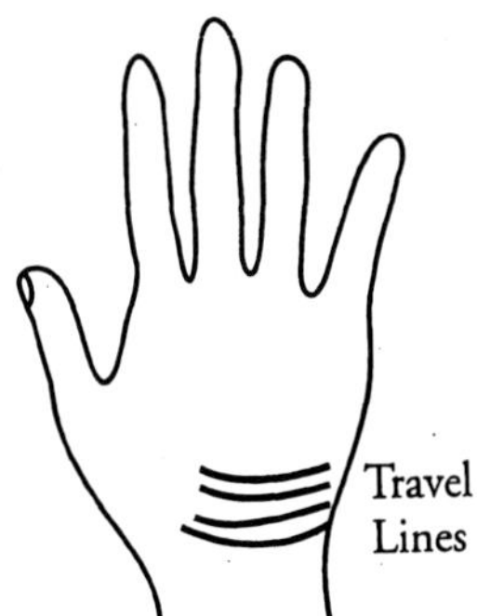

Travel Lines

The Travel Lines indicate major trips taken throughout your life.

They start from the edge of the palm opposite the thumb, and extend horizontally.

They pass over the Line of Moon or are seen proceeding from the area of Venus towards the area of Mars, and seen crossing the area of Dragon's Head, towards the Mount of Moon. Such lines are both thick and thin.

Horizontal lines from the outer edge of the hand indicate restlessness or a desire to travel.

If a Travel Line intersects the Fate Line, this is an indication that your travels will present a life-changing experience.

Breaks in the lines indicate a delay in your travels.

If a square appears on the lines, it is a sign of protection in your travels.

Lines that cross the Travel Line foreshadow danger, or problems with travel.

If a travel line intersects with the Life Line, then a trip will be made under circumstances of health, or your health will be affected by a trip.

The longer and stronger each line is, the more important the journey.

The Lines of Children

These lines are seen near the Mount of Mercury in the form of vertical lines over the marriage line. These lines are very thin and cannot be seen with the naked eye.

The Bracelets

The Bracelets, or Rascettes as they are also known, are the lines between the palm and the wrist.

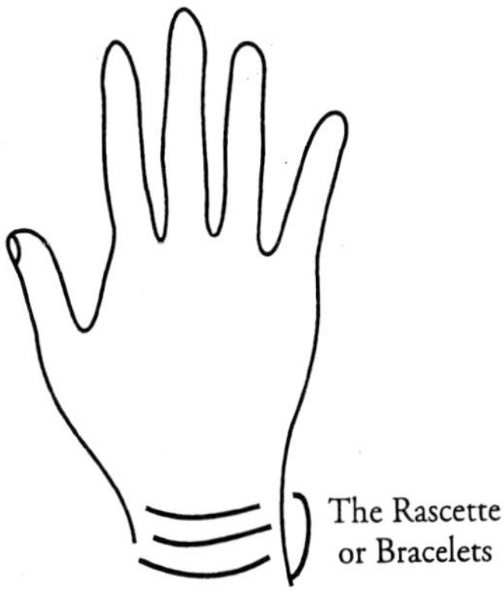

The Rascette or Bracelets

These lines are different in number in different hands. Some hands even have four lines.

A top rascette that is curved and pushed up towards the palm indicates there may be a weakness in the reproductive area.

Three strong rascettes may indicate a long life.

The Casual Lines

These lines are formed from time to time and show the bad and good times of a person. They are not permanent and disappear once the momentary influence is over. These lines form in different places on the palm.

The High Post Line

This line commences from the wrist and is seen proceeding towards the area of Dragon's tail. If this line is deep and distinct, the person shall certainly attain a great post in life.

The Line of Escape

People with this line like to escape from the problems in their lives. If the line connects with the Health Line this can mean that they tend to indulge in drugs and drinking.

The Line of Intuition

This line appears on the outer palm and highlights a strong insight. If you are lucky enough to have this line then you are sensitive, intuitive and may possess psychic powers.

The full line of intuition is often seen in people who are mediums, astrologers, palmists and those connected with healing and humanitarian people.

Via Lascivia

The Via Lascivia is a horizontal line across the Mount of Luna.

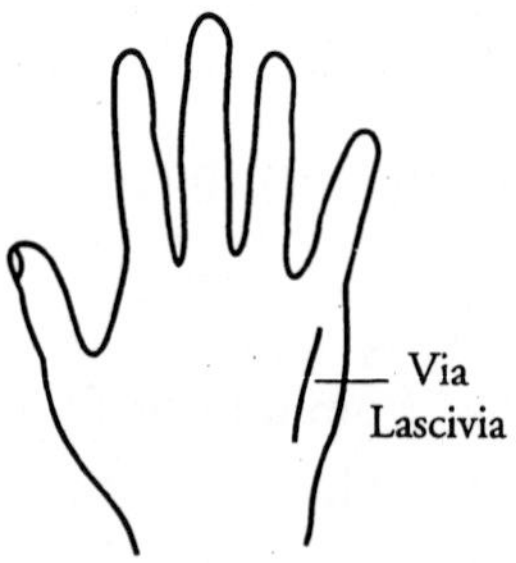

Via Lascivia

In the past it was thought to represent a promiscuous behaviour. These days it is linked to people who have a sensitivity to allergies.

Bow of Intuition

This is another rare marking.

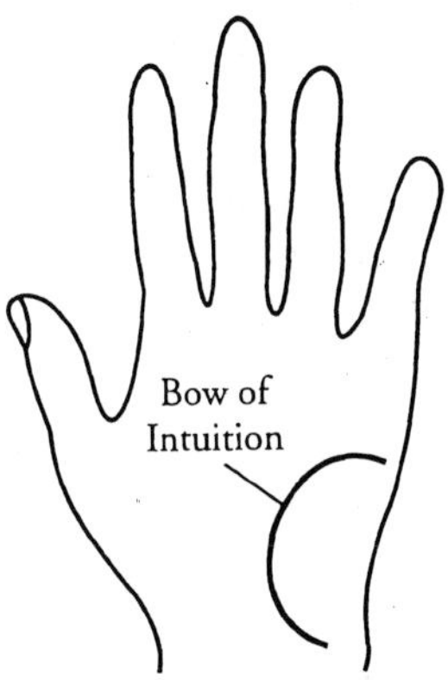

Bow of Intuition

It is found on the percussion side of the palm, starting on the Mount of Luna and curving round to beneath the Mercury finger.

Those who have this line have extraordinary intuition.

Ring of Solomon

The Ring of Solomon is found on the mount at the base of the Jupiter finger. It is also known as the Ring of Jupiter.

It is usually found on hands of people who have a good deal of common sense.

Those who posses this mark will make good politicians, teachers, lawyers and judges.

Simian Line

The Simian Line runs across the hand replacing the Heart and Head Lines. It is a sign of inner tension.

It may be destructive or creative or even both. It is interesting to note that people who tend to be religious fanatics tend to have a simian line.

Medicine has also found that Simian Lines may also be associated with certain types of heart defects. People with a Simian Line never really find peace. They spend their entire lives searching for an answer they never really find.

To the person with the Simian Line there is only right or wrong and nothing in between. People with this line work twice as hard, study twice as hard and fight twice as hard.

Medical Stigmata

There is a pattern often found on the hands of medical people. It is called the medical stigmata. It is a small patch of vertical lines beneath the little finger.

People with this marking are drawn to medical or social work.

It is very common on the hands of nurses yet less common on the hands of doctors. This is interesting because it shows that some doctors choose their career path for money and prestige whereas it tends to show that nurses are more emotionally involved in this choice of career.

A hand with the medical stigmata and many fine lines will turn towards social work. People who work in the natural therapies area also have this mark.

An unusual marking called the St Andrew cross is found on the hands of people who have saved the life of another.

Markings on Lines

Bracelet Lines

1. A star in the middle of the top Bracelet will forecast a legacy.
2. A cross in the same position indicates problems early on in adult life.
3. A Bracelet line that is chained indicates a life of struggle.
4. A Bracelet line with lots of islands shows a person who worries about life.

Line of Intuition

1. An island in the Line of Intuition will bring poor success.
2. An island at the beginning of the Line of Intuition may show someone who sleepwalks.
3. If the Line of Intuition ends in a star this person will have great success in life.
4. If the Line of Intuition merges into the Fate Line this person will have career success.

Line of Mars

1. If the Mars Line cuts across the Line of Success that has a dot or cross at the end of the line, the reputation of this person will be destroyed.

2. If the Line of Mars ends on the Mount of the Moon with a cross, dot, or star this person may die of alcohol or drug abuse.
3. If the Line of Mars ends on the Mount of the Moon with a star, dot or cross, and the Head Line ends in a star, this person will have a mental breakdown at the time the star appears on the Head Line.

Line of Influence

1. A star at the end of the Line of Influence shows the end of that influence.
2. If the Line of Influence crosses the Life or Head Line and a red dot is formed, a major illness or accident is formed.
3. A Worry Line that starts from a star on the end of a Line of Influence and cuts past the Life Line indicates a death of a relative at that time in the Life Line.

Line of Marriage

1. An island on the Marriage Line will show an unhappy marriage.
2. When the Marriage Line ends in a star it indicates the marriage will end in an explosive situation.
3. If there are branches on the under side of the Marriage Line it shows a marriage of heartbreak.
4. If there are branches that rise from the Marriage Line it will show a very happy marriage.

Line of Success

1. Islands on the Line of Success indicate serious problems such as a major loss of money.
2. Dots on the Line of Success indicate loss of name.
3. Cutting bars on the Line of Success cause setbacks in your career.

Ring of Saturn

1. When there is a Ring of Saturn and the Fate Line has a dot, cross or star, it indicates this person's career may be ruined through lack of concentration.
2. If a person has a Ring of Saturn with a Head Line that slopes low on the Mount of Moon which is large and grilled, it will show this person will have a great imagination.
3. If the Ring of Saturn is composed of two lines that form a cross on the Mount of Saturn it is not a good sign as it may indicate this person has a suicidal tendency.

Defective Lines

An uneven line is a defective line that can be seen on any line.

The uneven line can be deep, then become thin and continue that way the length of the line.

A broad and shallow line indicates a person who is uncertain with very poor self-control.

Capillary lines are finely traced lines that run together, eventually uniting into one line.

When a mount has a capillary line it will mean the power of the mount is lessened.

Wavy lines indicate a person who lacks the decision-making ability. These people are followers, not leaders.

A tassel, a group of lines extending from the end of a line, is always a defect and will mark the end of the usefulness of a line.

Broken lines are seen often and are indicative of a defective condition.

The kind of break of a line indicates the outcome of the defect.

A chained line is always a very serious defect and hard to repair.

CHAPTER-11

THE MARKINGS ON THE PALM

Every human hand contains good or bad signs, which are important to the general behaviour of the lines on the palm and mounts.

In addition to the major and minor lines of the hand there are various other markings. Not all these appear on every individual's hand but they contribute to a greater understanding of the hand.

Grilles

The grille is a point at which the energies of the hand dissipate or escape out. The grille is very often seen, and generally upon, the mounts of the hand. If grilles are found throughout the entirety of the hand, the power of its bearer is constantly drained by vexations and imagined slights.

These represent a destructive force, as the lines do not go anywhere. They ultimately take away the power from the line. A grille on the first finger suggests possessiveness and greed, on the little finger, dishonesty.

If a grille appears on the mount, it saps or thwarts the qualities of the mount, e.g. such a grille on the Mount of Apollo will forever put off the attainment of any true success in life.

The Grille

A grille on the Mount of Jupiter denotes egotism, pride and dominative spirit.

A grille on the Mount of Apollo represents vanity, folly, and a desire for celebrity.

A grille on the mount of mercury represents an unstable and rather unprincipled person.

A grille on the Mount of Saturn represents misfortune, a melancholy nature and morbid tendency.

A grille on Mount of Venus represents caprice in passion.

A grille on the Mount of Luna foretells restlessness, discontent, and disquietude.

Bars and Circles

These are quite rare but often appear on lines as islands. A circle on the Apollo Mount by the end of the Apollo line shows brilliance. If it appears anywhere else then this is an unfortunate mark.

Bars

Bars and dots always mean a hindrance, with dots having a lesser negative effect.

Bars

The Life-saving Cross

Crosses always denote troubles, disappointment, danger, and when found on lines, the harm to the bearer may be aggravated, as the Holy Cross of Jesus Christ.

Occasionally it can refer to a dramatic change in one's life due to a crisis or hardship. They should always be considered an ill omen save for two cases: when found on the Mount of the Jupiter and when located between the Head and Heart Lines, known as the "**Croix Mystique**". If you have this marking between the Life and Fate Lines about 4-6 cm from the wrist, this mark may not mean that you literally save lives but shows someone who often works to help others, for example, doctor, nurse or teacher. The bearer of such a symbol is purported to possess a greater degree of mysticism, occultism, and superstition.

The Cross

If the cross is opposite to a star, it is considered as a fovourable sign.

Stars

The star is a symbol of good and sudden brilliance in a person's life. A star on the hand emphasizes incidents. If it is separate and independent, it is powerful. Its position in the hand will indicate whether it is good or bad.

A star is formed of three or more lines cutting each other at a point and forming at least fine, clear radii. It is representative of the fusion of life current at a point.

A star on a line, or at the end of a line, warns of impending events for good or evil.

A star near the end of the Life Line denotes some shock and should be a warning sign.

A star on the Head Line denotes a poor decision-making ability or an accident to the head.

A star on the Heart Line spells emotional troubles.

At the end of the Fate or the Sun Line, it indicates success after long periods of hard work.

A star on the Life Line means potential personal injury.

The Star

A line that ends in a star signifies the greatest accomplishments possible; however, the star often carries with it an unpleasant price. For example, if the Line of Apollo ends in a star, it denotes great fame, but this often results in the person suffering the loss of privacy due to becoming a successful public figure.

A star on the mounts will naturally denote great proficiency with the mount's corresponding traits, yet these traits may consume some of the other bearer's qualities. The star is certainly a sign to be viewed with great caution.

A star on the top of the Mount of Jupiter along with a good Head Line shows the acquisition of great honour and position.

If the star is found without a good Line of Head, it predicts a head injury or an operation for tonsillitis or separation from wife in old age.

When the star is at the base of the mount, the person has contacts with rich and eminent people.

If there is a star in the left hand on the Mount of Jupiter, the native is born with a silver spoon in his mouth and will achieve a good position in life. If the Life Line is joined to the star on this mount, the native will achieve success by his intellectual ability.

A star on the Mount of Jupiter signifies great honour, power and position.

A star on the Mount of Apollo gives wealth and position but without happiness.

A star on the Mount of Mercury represents success in science, the power of eloquence.

A star on the Mount of Mars denotes that through patience, resignation and luck great honours would be gained.

A star on the Mount of Saturn represents great success or distinction through some terrible fate.

A star on Mount of Venus represents extraordinary success in all affairs of love.

A star on Mount of Luna is a sign of great celebrity status.

The Croix Mystique

This cross is found beneath the middle finger between the Head and Heart Lines, and shows a distinct interest in occult matters.

The position of the "**Croix Mystique**" is also quite important. If located high up, near the Mount of Jupiter, the person will exhibit belief in mysticism only for his own gain.

Those with crosses further from the Mount of Jupiter will care more for the principles and methods by which the mystical experience was expressed rather than its immediate application to themselves.

Transverse Marks

A transverse line marking on the hand is an evil sign that nullifies the positive qualities of any mount it is found upon. Though a person may have the markings of a good mount, these qualities can be reduced if it has a score of transverse lines.

If transverse lines are found across the Mount of Mercury, it indicates that the bearer will use his talents of diplomacy and tact for deceit and guile for ill gains.

Vertical Marks

Vertical markings are a benefic sign. If found on the mounts, they heighten its positive qualities and assist in annulling any poor signs also located on the mount. They are the opposites of the aforementioned transverse markings.

Vertical markings upon the Mount of Mercury will bring a great deal of tact and loquaciousness to serve for pleasant communication and friendship. It will emphasize science and business skills.

Two vertical lines on the Mount of Mercury are often the symbol of a doctor or biologist.

The Island

An island is always a negative sign. It is gradual and prolonged, and oft times subtle period of strife in an individual's life. It is often a sign of some hereditary evil, such as a heart condition or intemperance with spirits, but it may just as easily represent non-congenital emotional stress.

It could represent mounting stress on the line of the head, and manifest itself as headaches.

On the Line of Fate, it could be a period in which the individual finds himself surrounded with mounting debts that peak at the widest point of the island. These misfortunes will last to the extent that the island is long.

The Island

It denotes inherited heart disease if heavily marked on the Line of Heart.

It could represent mounting stress on the Head Line, and manifest itself as headaches.

An island on a mount injures the qualities of the mount on which it is found.

An Island on the Mount of Jupiter weakens one's pride and ambition.

An island on the Mount of Apollo weakens the talent for art.

An island on the Mount of Mercury makes a person too changeable for him to succeed, anything related to business or science.

An island on the Mount of Mars represents a weak spirit and cowardice.

An Island on the Mount of Saturn brings misfortune to the person.

An island on the Mount of Venus leads a person to easily be influenced by the sport of fancy and passion.

An island on Mount of Luna shows the weakness in working out the power of the imagination.

The Square

The square is usually called "The mark of preservation". The line denotes one of the greatest crises in the person's life. It is almost always a benefit symbol. It denotes an especial significance when covering an area that is experiencing turmoil, such as chained, broken, or dotted lines. In this instance, difficulties will arise but the person will persevere and the crisis will be averted or thwarted. Damage may be reduced to a minimal one or prevented altogether.

A square after perturbations in a line signifies repair. The one instance in which the square denotes negative influences is when it is found on the upper portion of the Mount of Venus near the Life Line, where it denotes detention or incarceration.

The Square

It denotes negative influences when it is found on the upper portion of the Mount of Venus near the Life Line.

A square on the Mount of Jupiter signifies ambition of the person.

A square on the Mount of Apollo provides a desire for fame.

A square on the Mount of Mercury provides a restless, mercurial temperament.

A square on the Mount of Mars denotes danger through enemies.

A square on the Mount of Saturn represents fatality that shadows the life.

A square on the Mount of Venus denotes preservation from trouble brought on by passion. In the centre of the Mount it shows that the person will fall in danger but always manage to escape.

A square on the Mount of Luna represents excess of imagination.

The Circle

The circle is a very rare marking in palmistry. It is an evil mark unless it is on a mount, in which case it usually augments the powers and promise of a mount.

If it touches any line, it brings inescapable misfortune to the line it touches. The person would go round and round in a circle without being able to breakthrough and get free out of life's hassles.

The Circle

If it is found on the Mount of Apollo it is fortunate and on any other mounts it goes against success.

When it touches any important line, it indicates that at that particular point the subject will not be able to clear himself from misfortune.

A circle on the Mount of Luna represents danger from drowning.

The Triangle

The triangle is a curious sign, and it is clear and distinct and not formed by chance crossing of lines. It denotes mental flourish and success corresponding to the location of the mark.

It is a positive sign, though a strong significance should be ascribed to it only when it stands as an independent mark, not composed of intersecting lines.

It denotes mental flourish and success corresponding to the location of the mark, i.e., if it were to be found upon the Mount of Apollo, it would denote an artistic success. If it is alongside a line, it will naturally take on the significance dependent upon the line.

The triangle will never reach the great heights of success, but it possesses balance and will not carry with it the backlash that so often accompanies the star.

The Triangle

A triangle on the Mount of Jupiter signifies promises more than the usual success in the management of people, handling of men and organisational affairs.

A triangle on the Mount of Apollo denotes a practical application of art and a calm demeanour toward success and fame.

A triangle on the Mount of Mercury represents qualities and promises success in relation to business, finance and money.

A triangle on the Mount of Mars denotes science in warfare, great calmness in any crisis, and presence of mind in danger.

A triangle on the Mount of Saturn gives a talent and inclination for mystical work, for dēlving into occult study of human magnetism, etc.

A triangle on the Mount of Venus represents calmness and calculation in love, power of restraint and control over self.

A triangle on the Mount of Luna represents a scientific method in following out the ideas of imagination.

The Spot

A spot is a sign of a distinct event or malady, a sign of temporary illness, though it often comes in groups that denote a chronic disorder. It denote a chronic disease.

If found on a line, it typically signifies a temporary illness corresponding to the line, e.g., a spot on the Line of Head indicates some violence to the head or brain fever.

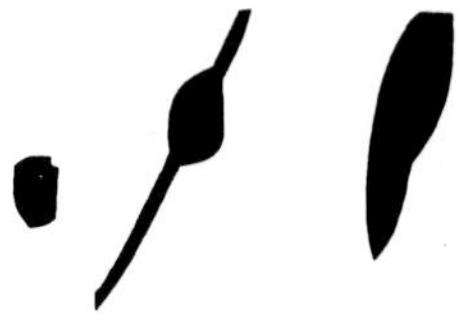

The Spot

Different colours of spot have their own meaning:

A bright red spot on the Line of Head signifies a shock or injury from some blow or fall. On the Line of Health, it represents illness and fever, and on the Line of Life is represents the nature of illness or fever.

A black or blue spot represents a nervous illness.

A spot on the Mount of Apollo represents a terrible sign of disappointment in the pursuit of fame, art or riches.

A spot on the Mount of Mars under Mercury denotes the dangerous opposition of enemies.

A spot on the Mount of Mars under Jupiter represents force, violence and even death from quarrels.

A spot on the Mount of Saturn, when touching the Line of Fate, denotes danger of violent death by accident, and in the centre of this mount, it increases the evil, fatalistic tendencies of the life.

A spot on the Mount of Venus represents great trial or fatal influence of affection; it shows troubles and quarrels with near relatives when it lies close to the Line of Life.

The Trident

The trident is a most propitious marking wherever it may lie. It is such a powerful symbol that it eclipses the star in beneficence.

Trident

If it rises from a line, it will expound the qualities of that line and draw additional power from the mounts or lines that branch on either side.

If it is on a mount, it carries with it a great flourish of the properties of that mount in conjunction with its neighbouring mounts.

The Tassel

A tasselled line can often be found at the end of the Life Line. As the person weakens and deteriorates with age, so too does the line.

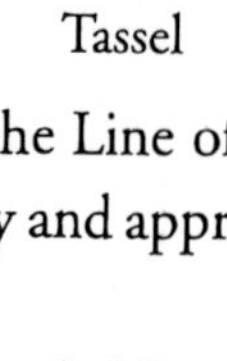

Tassel

Such is the case with the Line of Head, where it denotes a weakening of mental clarity and approaching senility or old age.

If it on the Line of Heart it denotes a deteriorating heart condition or emotional trauma that has left the person very feeble and unstable.

Drooping Offshoots

Lines that droop from any larger line indicate a disappointment in life.

Along thc Linc of Heart, it denotes disappointment in love or an unfortunate event in which the person becames too emotionally involved.

Along the Line of Head, it may signify the obstruction of one's ideals or disillusionment.

Rising Offshoots

Rising offshoots are the inverse of the drooping offshoots. They represent periods of sudden inspiration, fruition, and happiness.

A rising offshoot will draw upon the qualities of the mount that it is directed to. For example, an offshoot springing from the Line of Head and nearing the Mount of Mercury is a sign of scientific prowess—perhaps an invention, or a discovery, or a synthesis of concepts that have long been drifting through the person's mind, but had hitherto been dissociated.

Sister Lines

Sister lines support the line along which they follow.

Sister Lines

Some sister lines are quite common, such as the Line of Mars, which accompanies and strengthens the constitution denoted by the Line of Life.

The Line of Apollo is a sister line for the Line of Fate, as it serves a similar function and accentuates the fulfilment a person feels in the course of his career.

Sister lines protect and heal lines that are broken, crooked, frayed, or lie side-by-side.

If a line exists with several negative markings, sister lines will be the guiding hand that will shield the bearer from the brunt of life's assaults.

Palm Loops

Loop of Humour

This is found between the Apollo and Mercury fingers. It indicates a dry sense of humour.

Loop of Vocation

This is found between the Saturn and Apollo fingers. It reveals a strong dedication to work.

Raja Loop

An extremely rare marking found between the Saturn and Jupiter fingers, it indicates that there was royal blood in the person's family history.

Loop of Courage

This is found in the thumb joint, indicating a person of great courage.

Loop of Music

This loop sweeps in from the thumb edge onto the Mount of Venus. People who have this are natural musicians.

Loop of Inspiration

Rising from the wrist up the centre of the palm, it is often associated with poets.

Loop of Nature

This loop lies across the Mount of Luna. People with this loop have a strong connection with animals and nature.

Loop of Water

This flows down towards the Luna Mount. It indicates a strong affinity to water.

The Ridges

The Chinese have recognised the importance of ridges and used fingerprints for hundreds of years in many forms for various purposes. The first man to discover that the ridges on fingers and thumbs can be used for positive identification was Sir Henry

Faulds of England in 1880. In 1892, Sir Francis Galton, a famous scientist in England, proved that no two fingerprints are alike.

Ridges are classfied as:

Loop Type

Ridges run from one side to the other with an apex in the centre. It shows mental and emotional elasticity and versatility. If all the fingers bear this pattern, the person should control his feelings and diversification of interest.

Tented Arch

The tented arch is perpendicular to the ridges dropping on the sides like the canvas of a tent. Such persons are sensitive, susceptible to sound and fond of music. They should live in a peaceful environment. They have a highly-strung nervous system.

Arched

The apex flows across the finger like the lines of a little hump-backed hill. Such a pattern on fingers shows a dominating tendency and a suspicious, obstinate and hesitant nature. Digestive weakness and faulty blood conditions are also indicated.

Whorl Type

Its apex is formed by a circular whorl. It shows independence of thought and action. Such persons possess originality of thought but are suspicious. They become conventional to suit their convenience. They have a secretive attitude and do not want to discuss their plans with others. They may suffer from nervous digestive functioning or faulty heart action.

Composite Type

This type is formed by two curves or apexes running in a looped formation in inverse directions. This type has a practical and material bent of mind. There is some confusion in the mind due to the slow assimilation of theoretical abstraction. Such a person is medically predisposed to a fatty condition of the body.

Markings on the Plain of Mars

Many fine lines on the Plain of Mars indicate a person with a sudden temper.

A double trident indicates a person gifted in the arts.

A cross shows a person who tends to argue a lot.

Markings in the Great Triangle

A cross in the Great Triangle indicates an argumentative person.

A star indicates great success.

A grille in the Triangle indicates hidden enemies.

A circle in the Triangle indicates problems with the opposite sex.

Markings in the Quadrangle Area

When a clear psychic cross in the Quadrangle is not touching any line this person will be a very gifted psychic.

If there are crisscross lines or other defective signs this will cause restlessness in the person.

A star in the Quadrangle is a good sign and indicates outstanding success.

CHAPTER-12

HEALTH

For centuries medicine has recognised the link between palmistry and health. Modern medical researchers have confirmed this link. Given below are some of their findings.

Earth Hand

Susceptible to bowel or intestine problems.

Air Hand

Nervous tension and lung problems.

Fire Hand

Accidents and heart problems.

Water Hand

Allergies, nervous system and psychological problems.

Thick Palms

Thick, well-padded palms denote a robust constitution.

Thin Palms

Thin, fragile hands indicate a fragile constitution.

Markings on the Fingertips

Short dashes may indicate stress, while short vertical lines may indicate hormonal problems.

Forefinger

Pituitary gland

Middle Finger

Pineal gland

Ring Finger

Blood pressure

Little Finger

Thyroid

Health Markings

Islands on Heart Line

Beneath Saturn it may indicate hearing defects.

Laddered Heart Line

Beneath Apollo finger it may indicate calcium imbalance.

Star on the Line

A star on the Heart Line may indicate heart problems.

Keratoses

It may indicate an organ disease.

Diamond

A diamond attached to the Life Line may indicate gynaecological problems.

Tassel

Tasselling of Head or Life Line may indicate energy problems.

Fingernails

Speckles

Imbalance of zinc.

Vertical Ridges

Intestinal problems.

Horizontal Ridges

Trauma.

Wraparound

Respiratory problems.

Convex

Anaemia.

Fan-shaped

Need to relax.

Heart Problems

Short nails are often found among people with a history of heart problems.

Arch fingerprints are also associated with people who have heart problems and high blood pressure.

The Simian Line is also associated with people who may have heart problems.

If the Heart Line also has pronounced chaining it may indicate heart problems.

A complete breaking up and fragmenting at the end of the Heart Line often occurs in people before a heart attack.

CHAPTER-13

WEALTH AND SUCCESS

How wealthy will you be? The money lines don't indicate material wealth but point to that person having the skill to acquire cash and how it can be done.

Can wealth be detected in the hand? This all depends on which element you fall under.

Air Signs

Those with Air hands enjoy money and possessions when they have done it their way.

Fire Signs

Fire-handed people love luxury and wealth and everything has to be of the best.

Earth Signs

Earth types enjoy reaping their benefits from using their hands to create things.

Water Signs

If you have a Water sign then you will gain success in the entertainment business.

Here are some pointers to see just how much money will be coming your way! The more of these you have the better off you'll be.

1. Look for a wide/open hand with straight fingers.
2. A line travelling from the base of the thumb to the little finger indicates wealth acquired by inheritance.
3. Wide spacing between third and fourth fingers is a sure of success in anything you do.
4. A low set Head Line is an indication of great success.
5. A cross on the Mount of Jupiter shows unearned money will fall in your lap and a Saturn finger (shorter than first and third fingers) shows a gambling nature.
6. A star attached to the Apollo Line indicates a major win of money.
7. If a star is found on the Jupiter Mount it indicates good fortune, marriage into money and attainment of a position of importance in life.
8. A star on the Apollo Mount indicates the person has talents which will bring the owner fame and fortune. It is often found on the hands of successful actors. The star is the most important indication of luck to be found in your hands, but only when it is found on the upper Mounts of Jupiter, Mercury or Apollo, at any point along the Apollo Line or at the top of the Fate Line.
9. A trident sign at the end of the Fate Line is a sign of material success.

10. A line that runs from the base of the thumb to below the index finger ending in a star indicates a natural talent for moneymaking.
11. A line running from the base of the thumb to below the middle finger indicates money made in business.

Career

Often young people go to see palmists seeking answers about the right career choice. It must be noted that if a person is truly dedicated to succeed in a career choice they will do so even if their palms may disagree. Palmistry does not take away free will.

But in the study of palmistry, what happens when we see people with a missing fate line? These people have a somewhat unique nature about them. Often they will change jobs several times in their life. Their life is never settled and they shift around a lot.

But how can palmistry help the employer find the right employee? Well, the simplest way is to look at the fingers. If they lie close together it shows a hard-working stable employee. But if there are wide gaps between the fingers it may show an employee that will cause problems.

Retirement in the Hands

People with Earth hands find retirement very difficult and usually prefer to work until the end.

Air hand people on retirement like to get involved in activities such as study and groups.

On retirement people with Fire hands tend to join clubs and community projects.

People who have a Water hand enjoy retirement and are happy to lie around reading, watching television and pursue other such interests.

The quality of your retirement can be found in the top most sections of the Fate and Apollo Lines and the end of the Life Line. About the last two-fifths of the Life Line represent the retirement years.

Islands represent ill health while branches suggest new journeys, and a neat, strong ending shows vitality.

On retirement the Fate Line usually shows a break. Islands warn of financial problems while branches show new interests.

An Apollo Line above the Heart Line indicates happiness in old age, especially if it is strong.

Three parallel lines indicate financial success.

Only long lines relate to marriages, the short ones to deep affection or marriage.

Some of variations of this line and its representations are discussed below.

1. When the Marriage Line lies close to the Line of Heart, the union will be early, about fourteen to twenty.
2. When it is near the centre of the mount, then marriage may take place at about twenty-one or twenty-eight years of age.
3. When it is three-quarters up the mount, twenty-eight to thirty-five and so on.
4. When the girdle goes over the side of the hand and comes in contact with the Line of Marriage, the happiness of the marriage will be marked through the peculiarities of the temperament. Such subjects are peculiarly exciting, and hard to live with. If on a man's hand, that man would want as many virtues in a wife as there are stars in the universe.

An island on the Marriage Line will show an unhappy marriage.

When the Marriage Line ends in a star it indicates the marriage will end in an explosive situation.

If there are branches on the underside of the Marriage Line it shows a marriage of heartbreak.

If there are branches that rise from the Marriage Line it will show a very happy marriage.

The number of lines in a female's palm reflect the number of possible children including abortion, miscarriages, even of the little periods when a woman is not knowledgeable of her pregnancy. The lines of male represent the number of real children.

Signs of Widowhood

A black dot on the Marriage Line shows widowhood.

A break in the Marriage Line may indicate the sudden death of the partner.

When the Marriage line ends with a star on the Mount of Mercury it shows death of the partner.

When a Marriage Line is cut at its termination by another line it shows the death of the partner.

However, broken lines will lead to a separation for you. If your Affection Line curves down you will outlive your partner.

A fork at the end of the Marriage Line, toward the palm, indicates separation (with or without divorce).

Engagement

A line with a fork at the start, toward the back of the hand, indicates a long engagement.

Travel

The Travel Lines indicate major trips taken throughout your life. They start from the edge of the palm opposite the thumb, and extend horizontally. They are horizontal lines that enter the palm from the percussion edge.

These lines pass over the Line of Moon or seen proceeding from the area of Venus towards the area of Mars, crossing the area of Dragon's Head, and moving towards the Mount of Moon. Such lines are both thick and thin.

They lie across the Luna Mount and Mars Negative Mount.

The longer and stronger each line is, the more important is the journey.

People with an Earth hand tend to return to the same travel destinations each time rather than explore new places.

People with Air hands love travel and tend to pursue careers in the travel industry.

Fire hand people are adventurous and like to explore new places.

Water hand people like to travel to mystical and spiritual places.

Islands or stars on the Travel Lines on the edge of the Luna Mount are indications of problems. Islands tend to indicate the holiday was not as enjoyable as planned.

Stars on the Travel Line indicate great danger.

Horizontal lines from the outer edge of the hand indicate restlessness or a desire to travel.

If a Travel Line intersects the Fate Line, this is an indication that your travels will present a life-changing experience.

Breaks in the lines indicate a delay in your travels.

If a square appears on the lines, it is a sign of protection in your travels.

Lines that cross the Travel Line foreshadow danger, or problems with travel.

If a Travel Line intersects with the Life Line, then a trip will be made under circumstances of health, or your health will be affected by a trip.

❑❑❑